...ONAGHY

UNZIPPED

everything teenagers
want to know about
love, sex and each other

 H...

...*bers*

To Kristine and Melanie, my brilliant, generous sisters, who – despite fairly impressive odds – have always helped me see the funny side of life.

HarperCollins*Publishers*

First published in Australia in 1999
Reprinted in 1999 (three times), 2000 (twice)
by HarperCollins*Publishers* Pty Limited
ABN 36 009 913 517
A member of the HarperCollins*Publishers* (Australia) Pty Limited Group
http://www.harpercollins.com.au

HarperCollins*Publishers*
25 Ryde Road, Pymble, Sydney, NSW 2073, Australia
31 View Road, Glenfield, Auckland 10, New Zealand
77-85 Fulham Palace Road, London W6 8JB, United Kingdom
Hazelton Lanes, 55 Avenue Road, Suite 2900, Toronto, Ontario M5R 3L2
and 1995 Markham Road, Scarborough, Ontario M1B 5M8, Canada
10 East 53rd Street, New York NY 10022, USA

The National Library of Australia Cataloguing-in-Publication data:

Donaghy, Bronwyn, 1948–   .
    Unzipped : everything teenagers want to know about love,
    sex and each other.
    Includes index.
    ISBN 0 7322 5780 8
    1. Sex instruction for youth. II. Title.
306.70835

Printed in Australia by Griffin Press on 79gsm Bulky Paperback

11 10 9 8 7 6
03 02 01 00

*Information on STDs and contraception was drawn primarily from material
published by Family Planning NSW. Statistics on teenage sexual habits were
provided by the Centre for the Study of Sexually Transmissible Diseases,
Faculty of Health Sciences, La Trobe University, Victoria.*

Extract from Growing Pains *by Dr David Bennett, Doubleday, 1995,
reprinted with permission.*

Extracts from 'Better Be Home Soon' by David Leser printed in Good Weekend,
June 20 1998, reprinted with permission.

CONTENTS

FOREWORD

Adolescent sexuality is a complex and confronting subject. It is an enormously important subject. Impossible to avoid, as an integral and inescapable part of living, but difficult to embrace with equanimity, because its downside is so scary, it demands our attention and deserves our understanding. Adolescent sexuality needs to be back on the national agenda!

Unzipped: Everything Teenagers Want to Know About Love, Sex and Each Other tells the contemporary story of adolescent love, lust and longing. It speaks directly to young people as well as to all interested and caring adults. In a style uniquely her own, author Bronwyn Donaghy explores the diverse landscape of sexual feelings and expression, deftly sifting through the minefield of fact and fable. Nothing is glossed over. Little of substance is left out.

Within these riveting pages, certain truths may be found shocking, while others will be warmly reassuring to everybody. It is no surprise to learn, for example, that teenage sex is rarely 'romantic like in the movies'. In reality, it is more likely to be messy, quick and disappointing. Both boys and girls, to varying degrees, tend to get sex and love mixed up. And, of course, where one's sexuality is concerned, there are all the potential threats to health, happiness and even life itself. On the other hand, 'It is absolutely possible for two young people to have a loving relationship without having sex.' This is an important message, to do with the benefits of taking things slowly, if possible, and of being aware that there is so much more than sexual intercourse (whatever the gender mix) in the making of a mature and intimate friendship between two people.

As was the case with *Anna's Story* (about the untimely ecstasy-related death of Anna Wood in 1995) and *Leaving Early* (about the tragedy of youth suicide in Australia), Bronwyn Donaghy brings us the candid voices of real young people. They are your children's peers or people your children know. Experiences related to sexual initiation, identity confusion, uncertainty and regret sit alongside those reflecting love, courage, resilience and hope. And, without exception, the crucial role that parents can and should play, through their concern, guidance and support, quietly resonates through.

More than ever before, young people need a realistic perspective on themselves as sexual beings as they attempt to find their way through a jungle of hormonal drives, peer pressure and media hype. This book delivers just that. Please read it, think about it, talk about it and promote it to others who might benefit.

Clinical Associate Professor David Bennett
Head, Department of Adolescent Medicine
New Children's Hospital, Westmead, New South Wales

AUTHOR'S
ACKNOWLEDGMENTS

I am very grateful to the following people, who assisted me with my struggle through the maze of myths, folklore, scandals, misconceptions, research, passions, prejudice, facts and opinions, both academic and otherwise, and, inevitably, the moral issues that surround the subject of adolescent sex and sexuality:

Dr Melissa Kang, for her time, her knowledge, her patience and tolerance – no wonder the kids trust her so much; Associate Professor David Bennett, Head of the Department of Adolescent Medicine and the Director of the NSW Centre for the Advancement of Adolescent Health, New Children's Hospital, and consultant family therapist Dr Michael Reed for making this project possible; Dr Simon Clarke, from Westmead Hospital, who always has just the right words; Shane Brown, from South Sydney Youth Services – I wonder if his young clients know how lucky they are to call him a friend; and Julia Tresidder for steering me in the right direction.

Kaaren Dudley, from Nepean District Hospital, whose devotion to her young pregnant couples is unquestionable; the Youth Team from Family Planning NSW for their practical advice and for allowing me to draw heavily from their excellent publications; Professor Doreen Rosenthal from the Centre for Sexually Transmissible Diseases, La Trobe University; Karen Shea from the National Children's and Youth Law Centre; and Dr Mira Vellani.

Professor Sol Gordon, one of America's most eminent scholars and a leading sex educator, whose love for young people and practical wisdom have been my inspiration while writing this book.

Dr Alvera Stern, from Macro International in the United States, for her contribution on the subject of sex and drug abuse.

The young people – 'Hannah', 'Jake', 'Amira', 'Kim', Helen', 'Raymond' 'Gerry' and 'Julia' – you know who you are and how grateful I am for your honesty. Without these young people's contributions, this would be just another textbook.

Finally, my editors, Robin Freeman and Carolyn Leslie, for their patience; my friends Jennie Orchard and Angela Wood for their wise advice and constant encouragement; and my family, for passing another endurance test – in particular my younger son and his fourteen-year-old friends, who, when I begged them in desperation for some comments on masturbation, fixed their gentle eyes on mine and said: 'Mrs Don . . . Do NOT go there.'

Okay, boys, I won't. But I'm going just about everywhere else.

So now read on. You might even learn something you don't already know.

I did.

Bronwyn Donaghy

'What's missing from sex education is an honest study and discussion of love and intimacy. How can you teach kids about sex if they haven't first learned about love?'

Professor Sol Gordon.

'... full attention should be given to the promotion of mutually respectful and equitable gender relations and particularly to meeting the educational and service needs of adolescents to enable them to deal in a positive and responsible way with their sexuality.'

United Nations – International Conference on Population and Development, 1994.

'Any twelve-year-old who knows the clitoris is purely for pleasure is a lot wiser than her mother.'

From *Keeping Mum: Secrets of Happy Parenting and Other Lies*
by Bronwyn Donaghy.

When he reached the top of the stairs she was there. She was one of the girls clustered like bunches of navy-blue berries around the doorway to the classroom. All around her the others talked, cackled, leaned up against the prison-brick walls, sloppy, noisy, knowing, some slyly staring, but most of them not noticing him at all. Lucy was different. She wasn't so much leaning on the wall as tilting against it, holding her slender body in a straight, but slanting, line. She was such a nice shape for a girl, he thought, not bulky and busty but not a stick woman either. She wasn't talking at all. There was a dreamy look on her pale face but she suddenly turned her head and looked straight at him.

He was surrounded by rushing, crashing boys, heaving their backpacks off as they headed for class. They shouted and laughed and lunged at each other but Ben just stood there at the top of the stairs, looking at Lucy. And now she was looking back. The noise that surrounded them seemed to blur into a background roar and the kids were navy shadows, fading, moving in slow motion. It seemed for a long second as if Ben and Lucy were the only people there.

And then she smiled.

INTRODUCTION:
DISCOVERING SEX

There is nothing simple about sex.

Sexuality is as natural as the sea and as free as fresh air. Sex is essential for the creation of new life, for which the bodies of men and women have been perfectly designed. But sexuality is not just a biological phenomenon. It is a precious part of every single person on earth and it plays a crucial role in our commitment to one another. For most people, sex and sexuality are an important part of love and loving.

Sex is not just physical. But it is very physical. It is not driven purely by emotion. But it is very emotional. It's definitely not intellectual. And yet sex is so much better if the two people involved know and understand each other's needs and desires.

Having sex is not as ordinary as breathing, sleeping and eating. Sex doesn't happen just because the brain in the director's chair marshals the troops of body organs and orders them to do what they are told.

Sexuality takes the hearts and minds and spirits of two people and then briefly, powerfully, miraculously it physically unites them in an act more intimate than any other they will ever perform.

Sex is wonderful! But it's never simple.

For young people especially, sex is terribly complicated. Girls and boys growing up in a sex-minded, media-driven world are constantly confronted with sexual images and stories. Unfortunately, despite living in an information-obsessed society, they have no idea where to find the specific knowledge they need. Nobody really wants to talk to them about sex. Sex might sell millions of magazines each month and pulsate from television screens every night, but when young people need basic answers to basic questions they tend to turn to each other.

Few adults feel comfortable about getting down to the nitty-gritty of sexuality. A lot of parents are uncertain about the way they are conducting their own sex lives. Why would they want to tell kids how to do it?

It's not just the older generation who feel squeamish. Young people don't show much enthusiasm for discussing it either. Especially with people who probably don't do it any more.

Whether they talk in terms of dicks and cunts and fucking, or penises and vaginas and sexual penetration, nobody feels too good about putting the words to a useful purpose. It's not that we don't want them to know. It's not that they don't want to know. It's just that nobody wants to be the one to bring it up.

Young people are eager to believe that sex is joyful, passionate, mind-blowing, satisfying and terrific fun. The trouble is that for many of them sex turns out to be destructive, miserable, painful, confusing, annoying, frightening and ordinary.

They need to know why.

Young men and women need to know that during adolescence, sex is not an essential part of being in love. Thousands of them would almost certainly be infinitely relieved to learn that there are many ways other than having sex to express affection for someone they really like. But who knows how to take the pressure off them? Who will convince them of the good news – that there is nothing wrong but a good deal right about delaying their sex lives until they have survived all the other problems and confusions of adolescence?

Just in case they follow the example of previous generations and refuse to listen to advice from older and occasionally wiser mortals, young people need information. They should be provided with all the facts on sex and sexual activity so that if – *if* – they decide to try it for themselves, they will be well prepared, protected and safe.

Young girls, particularly those aged between thirteen and sixteen, are under a lot of pressure to have sex. If they do, they tend not to enjoy it much. They are not likely to be in a stable, mutually caring relationship and, apart from that, boys in that age group are not very good at sex. A young teenage boy having intercourse with a (usually even younger) girl will almost certainly ejaculate very quickly, plunging into her body with an urgency neither of them understands. Girls go along with sex because their boyfriends ask them to, because it's important for them to keep their boyfriend, and because their girlfriends say they should. Afterwards they worry – about getting pregnant, about their parents finding out, about whether the boy will still love them and, most of all, about what their friends will think of them now. For most young teenage girls, the approval of their friends is never guaranteed, but it is nevertheless more important to them than almost anything else.

Girls are still expected to be responsible for contraception. Girls who are economically or socially disadvantaged are still likely to become pregnant at an early age.

But boys are under pressure too. They are expected to dispense with their virginity as early as they can in order to demonstrate their masculinity. Boys who are having sex – or say they are – are still known as studs, although some youth workers believe that the double standard for both sexes may be changing. These days, boys as well as girls can be called sluts.

For young men, early sexual activity and promiscuity is closely linked to vandalism, truancy, drug abuse and binge drinking.

Despite the eloquent public voice of the gay and lesbian movement, young homosexual people are still suffering terribly and many of them are homeless as a result of admitting their sexual orientation. On the other hand, they are increasingly well tolerated by their peers, except in rural areas, where conformity, insularity and intolerance means homophobia is still a serious problem, along with widespread depression and a terrifyingly high rate of youth suicide.

Because of early sexual experimentation, many young people are confused and anxious about their sexual preference and unnecessarily guilt-stricken by their affection for same sex friends.

Adolescents are depicted in the media as being highly sensual beings. Movies, soap operas and commercials promote their message by portraying young men and young women as overtly sexual. Youth and beauty have always gone hand in hand, but the sexy image is one that has been created in the interests of commercial profit. Unfortunately, the kids find themselves under enormous pressure to fill the bill.

Adolescents' own expectations delude them as well. Even well-informed and educated young people expect sex to be like it is on the television, despite the fact that you can't tell from the screen version whether it's hurting, how it feels or what happens afterwards.

Because of what they've learned from the box, most young people think they know what is required of them – although there are exceptions. One fifteen year old told her midwife she hadn't realised she'd had intercourse until she became pregnant. 'I just lay there and he was doing this thing to me but I didn't know that was *it*.' Her boyfriend says he didn't know either. 'I thought it wasn't the real thing because she just lay there. On TV the girls move and make noises.'

There are uglier expectations. Some boys believe sex with their girlfriends is their automatic entitlement, especially if they have been 'going out' for more than a few weeks. In reality, teenage couples no longer *go out* anywhere much at all. They just hang around together, in the school playground, at the shops, in the street and in each other's bedrooms.

There's no doubt that boredom can lead to sex. If there's nothing else to do, here's something that's free and forbidden, which means it must be fun. While they are doing it, sex makes some kids feel loved and wanted. Warm flesh, soft kisses, loving arms. When the clothes come off and they become aroused and passionate, this particular simple pleasure becomes much more complex.

Sexuality, when it sweeps into our lives, is like the ocean, rushing over us in waves, flinging us high, dumping us low, terrifying us with its power, carrying us forward, sometimes against our will, taking us out beyond our depth or leaving us behind, disappointed, yearning for something unidentified beyond our reach.

The process of learning about sexuality and sexual relationships is a voyage of discovery which is only possible when people talk about it first. Without discussing sexuality and the way people relate to one another, a young person cannot possibly work out for herself or himself what they believe is right.

If love and sex are never mentioned, kids swim out into the sexual sea in a mass of confusion. They don't know where they are heading, nor do they understand when it's wise to go against the tide or how to avoid the rips and currents.

If they have been forbidden from swimming in that sea altogether, sooner or later they are still likely to plunge into the water. Without information and understanding, in their ignorant and rebellious frame of mind, they are sure to risk swimming in the most dangerous places, without taking the precautions that more experienced and responsible swimmers take for granted.

In the imperfect world in which most of us live, where morality is mocked and virginity is shocking, even young people know you can have good sex without love. Unfortunately, not even the virgins are convinced that you can have good love without sex.

What would they do if we shouted it from the tops of the city towers? What would happen if planes wrote it in swirling white letters across a wide blue sky . . .

HEY KIDS! IT'S OKAY NOT TO HAVE SEX!

Would they look up? Would they listen?

Lucy lay in bed and imagined what might have happened if only Ben had smiled back at her. Why hadn't he smiled? How hard could it be? What was wrong with her? What was wrong with him? If he wasn't interested enough to smile, why did he stand there for so long, just looking. Staring straight at her as if he was thinking of...what?

She closed her eyes. He could have smiled. And then she would have pushed herself off the wall and walked slowly towards him. And he would have moved towards her. And they would have stood together, their eyes locked for a long minute, and then they would have kissed. And the music in the background would have enveloped them and the kiss would have gone on and on...

And then she would have curled her arms around his neck and he would have moved his hands – those big, long-fingered hands that she watched in maths class as he jabbed away at his calculator – over her back and down to her bum, and he would have pressed her against him and the kiss would get deeper and she would open her lips a little and...

She opened her eyes. Under the sheets, she was caressing herself softly with spread fingers. It felt nice. But there was something wrong with her fantasy. This love scene was being played out in school uniform, with all those noisy boys and smart-arse girls crowding around, perving on them. Quite revolting. She closed her eyes again and moved the whole scene to a beach. She would be walking along the beach, collecting shells, and when she looked up Ben would just be standing there, gazing at her with that same expression he had worn at the top of the stairs. And they would move towards each other and...

She opened her eyes. The nearest beach was forty-five minutes' drive, more than an hour in weekend traffic. Why on earth would Ben turn up on the same beach, on the same day?

She took her hand out of her pyjama pants and crossed her arms behind her head. Shit! Even her dreams were impossible.

HANNAH'S STORY

The house where Hannah lives with her parents is high on a hill. On one side is the town; on the other is a valley, thickly wooded with trees which sway and ripple in the wind like a flying green carpet. Inside the cosy living room there are rustic cabinets with stained glass doors and deep, shabby, blissfully comfortable arm chairs.

Hannah is burning rosemary, sage and lemon oil to calm her and help her think. She is slight and slender, pale and pretty, with sky-blue eyes which crinkle when she laughs. She laughs a great deal, happy, hearty laughter which is the best sign of all that she's feeling a lot better than she used to. She regularly yanks her silky sweep of strawberry blonde hair out of its ponytail, and then ties it up again as she speaks.

The framed photographs on the mantlepiece are all of Hannah. Hannah as a little girl, hugging her Dad; Hannah the school girl with an arm slung around her mother's neck; Hannah looking like an ethereal princess, dressed up for her Year Twelve formal. Hannah and Dean, the golden girl with the dark and handsome boy – Barbie and Ken. Every fifteen minutes the clock beside the photographs chimes away the hours of a young life which in eighteen years has already seen a great deal of pain. But as Hannah is quick to point out, she's had a huge share of love as well.

'I love this house; I've lived here since I was two years old. There's me and Mum and Dad, and Gran lives in a flat at the back, and there are three cats and some fish that are so different to most people's because they absolutely refuse to die.

My parents had to wait until I was born to come to Australia. They wouldn't issue a visa to an unborn child. So when we arrived I was seven weeks old. My Mum and Dad wanted so much to have children and there were a lot of miscarriages before me, but I was the only one who made it.

My dad is an engineer and he used to travel a lot. My mum always worked part-time as a nurse, but they organised it so that one of them was usually around to pick me up after school.

If it was Dad he would take me to his factory where they had a little room with a table and a chair and games for me to play. Mum and I used to spend a lot of time here at home in the garden. She loves sewing and we would make things – little mice in walnut shells and things like that.

The three of us always did things together. We had some great holidays, we always spent weekends together – we are a very, very close family. I never ever wanted my childhood to end. I enjoyed being a kid so much.

I wouldn't say Mum and Dad are easy-going. I've been brought up to respect my elders, things like that. They're not over-strict – Mum's brought me up to make my own decisions and to be independent but also to respect other people. I can't just say: 'I'm going out.' They have to know where I'm going and what time I'll be getting home and if it doesn't suit them they'll ask me to maybe do it next weekend instead. They remind me that there are things to do around the house and that jobs have to be done, whether I'm going out or not. But they love my friends and my friends love them – they come around just to see my parents.

When I was fourteen I caught Ross River fever – at least that's what they think it was. It might have been glandular fever because the symptoms are the same – swollen glands and total exhaustion and it affects the liver and spleen. I missed a whole term of school and then I ended up with clinical depression.

I was very sick for a long time. I wasn't well all through the last two years of school and I rarely went for a whole week. I picked up every germ going and just a cold would knock me around for a month. I couldn't do sport. I went down to forty-eight kilograms. My so-called friends would ring up and say: "We've heard you're anorexic – what are you *doing* to yourself?" and I'm like: "For Chrissake, I'm *sick*, can't you understand that?" Mum had to make my clothes for me because nothing I owned fitted.

I was very disappointed in my girlfriends – the whole time I was really sick, only one of them came to see me. They thought they would catch something. Being sick changed everything for me. I lost my friends. I felt really bad about myself for a long time. But while I was sick I got tired of people pushing me around so now I stick up for myself.

My best friend, Vivien, she stuck by me the whole time. And now, of course, I've got Dean, my boyfriend.

I love kids, I really do. That's why now that I've finished school, I'm studying to be an early childhood teacher. Also the part-time curriculum I've chosen means I can do a lot of it at home, even if I'm sick in bed, which I sometimes still am. This way I can keep on working at getting better.

I remember when I was about eight, this boy saying "I'll show you mine if you'll show me yours." Him and his friend came over and I just sat there and had a look and thought: "Oh yeah, whatever – that's heaps good." Mum came up to see if we would all like a drink and she found me sitting there with them with my undies around my knees and she sent them away, but I didn't get into trouble. I didn't think it was naughty or bad, because we were a very open family. Mum and Dad used to wander from the bathroom to the bedroom without clothes on.

She just said I shouldn't do that again.

A while after that they bought *Where Did I Come From?* and Mum sat down with me and we went through it together and talked about it. I used to pull it out every now and again and have a squiz, a bit of a read.

I remember putting my arm up at school when I was about eleven and seeing a hair under my arm and the next birthday my Mum gave me my first bra. I hid it, because Dad was there when I opened it and I was really embarrassed. I got my period when I was twelve and I was at an agricultural field day. I loved those days – we'd go out to a property and we kids used to run riot, we'd go horse riding and we'd eat all the free honey and corn and these delicious potato patties. Anyway, all they had there were portaloos. A field full of portaloos. And I went for a wee and I thought: "*Eergh*! *What's that?*" Then I raced out and told my girlfriend that I'd got my period. I hadn't wanted to start, because that would mean if I had sex I could get pregnant. But once I started I felt so good. I felt really special. None of my friends had started and it wasn't awful. I never got any pain.

So I started growing up even though I didn't want to. But the idea grew on me – it had to happen.

I had my first boyfriend when I was eight, and we secretly held hands under the table. He's the biggest *dork* now. In

Year Five I had two boyfriends. One day we were on a bush walk and Simon was saying: "She's your girlfriend, why don't you kiss her?" and Donald says: "I don't know how." So Simon says: "I'll show you" and he grabs me and kisses me properly. Donald just said: "Ooh, wow." He was impressed. Then we walked home and I fell over and hurt my ankle so Simon had to give me a piggyback which impressed Donald even more.

By high school I was longing for a boyfriend, just so I could say I had one. It never happened. I had a couple of crushes at the school disco but they never got anywhere.

Josh was my first real boyfriend. We met when I was fourteen and he was sixteen; we were together for about sixteen months. We met at the skating rink. We started talking and phoning each other and one day we met at the local show. There was supposed to be a crowd of us but we were the only two who showed up. We were having a bucket of chips and a Coke and watching the fireworks and he asked me if I had a boyfriend and I said I didn't. So he said: "Well you've got one now if you want one."

He was a little podgy thing and he had pimples and tiny little eyes but he was a lovely person. I don't know what possessed me to get rid of him. I saw him the other day. He's lost his spots and he's tall and he's got muscles. He's turned out quite nice-looking after all.

Mum and Dad seemed all right about it. He was very shy. We didn't have our first kiss for three weeks. It was when we went to the movies – my parents drove me to his house and we went on the bus, in the middle of the day. I wasn't feeling very well – this was when I first started getting sick, but it wasn't diagnosed for two months. So we were sitting there in the movies and I was feeling sick and dizzy and he said: "Are you all right?" and I said: "Oh yeah, I guess," and then he just opened his mouth and clamped it on mine and jammed his tongue so far down my throat I nearly choked on it. I thought: "Eergh!" He goes: "You feel better now?" I said: "Oh sure." How could I say: "Well actually, now I feel even more like throwing up?" I felt sorry for him. He had never kissed a girl before. But it was revolting, it really was.

We went back to his house and he tried it again and that time I said: "No! That's not how it happens." He said: "Aren't I doing it right?" So I showed him. It all comes down to practice really. He was all right after that.

We were seeing each other for about four months before we had sex for the first time. I was sick for a lot of that time. But we used to muck around. He used to put his hand up my shirt and down my pants and that kind of stuff but it was never – neither of us ever got our clothes off. It's quicker to pull a shirt down than to have to put it on and his parents were always downstairs or mine were always around here. It's a bit risky to be taking all your clothes off when you are fourteen. We were just exploring and learning, I guess.

Having sex wasn't something that just happened. We talked about it for quite a while, wondering what it would be like. I don't know why we decided to go ahead with it. It was more his idea than mine but I wasn't under any pressure to do it with him. We actually planned the time and place. My parents had taught me to be a moral person, but they certainly didn't say that meant I couldn't have sex.

I was just starting to feel well again after having the fever and he had been really sweet to me the whole time and had visited me every day. I was so disappointed in everyone else. I think I was just thinking: "Anything goes." We were both awfully young.

It was the first time for both of us. We were alone at his place one day and he searched the whole house for a condom and he found one in his dad's room but it was two years out of date.

So Josh went off on his bike to the shops and I watched TV and waited for him. I wasn't nervous at all. He was really nervous when he got back. I put the condom on him. I didn't have any trouble – I just read the instructions on the packet. There was no foreplay.

We lay on the floor because he didn't want to get any stains on his bed cover. I didn't take my shirt off and neither did he. Just our pants.

I remember how much it bloody hurt!

I told him to stop after a few seconds because it hurt so much. I said: "Get off, I wanna watch tele." I got up and watched television for a while. About two hours later we tried again. He ejaculated that time.

Because he was so nervous it put a real dampener on the whole situation. There was nothing romantic about it at all. I think part of it was just knowing you were getting away with something.

In the following months I got very sick again. I also had a car accident and a couple of falls. I broke my leg. I spent months on crutches. It wasn't a good year, that's for sure.

Sex with Josh was never very good. He was a two-second wonder. After a while it became a bit of a bore. It didn't happen all the time, there weren't that many opportunities. We always used protection.

Every single time he would ask me: "Is it big enough for ya?" I'd always tell him it was. I mean, what difference did it make how big it was? It wasn't as if I had anything to compare it to!

More than having intercourse we used to play around with each other – handjobs are easier with parents around. I had this long body pillow on my bed so if Mum came in we would get that between us so she couldn't see that his pants were undone. Once he ended up with spermy stuff all over his shirt and he was walking down the hall to go home and I saw this huge wet patch, so I raced into the kitchen and got a glass of lemonade and pretended to spill it all over him. That was a good one, that was the best!

We tried oral sex a couple of times. I hated the smell and the taste but as long as I didn't have to swallow anything it didn't bother me too much. He did it to me first and I liked that a lot better than intercourse.

Josh did great massages – I love a massage. He was more interested in that, for some reason.

Anyway, it turned out Mum knew. Because I was having all these tests for my illness she saw my medical records. She asked me when did the sex start happening and I told her I couldn't remember. I couldn't, by then. She just said: "Oh well, at least you're using protection – I can't stop you" – and that was that.

Josh was obsessed with me. He did everything for me while I was sick. For my birthdays he would spend about $200. But one day we were just talking and he got angry and he went to hit me. He had never done that before and he didn't do it then but I thought next time he might, so I kicked him out. I said: "See ya" and that was that. He called me a stupid little bitch and things like that but it was only because he was so hurt.

I didn't have a boyfriend for about six months but during that time, when I was fifteen, I got in with a really rough crowd. We used to go out and get on to each other – just kissing and stuff. One of them left me with hickeys from here to here. But nothing below the waist, if you know what I mean.

Most of them were older and they took drugs. I smoked pot once with them. I hated it. They wanted to have sex but I wouldn't do it with any of them – they weren't the cleanest of people. I didn't know where they'd been before. Anyway, even though I didn't have much respect for myself at the time, because I'd been so sick and I felt so bad about everything, I never was a one-night-stand person. Those guys would certainly not have respected me afterwards, that's for sure.

Mum asked me about whether I was taking drugs, because I always smelled of them. I told her I had only smoked pot once and she had a bit of a cry and that was it. I think it helped that she found out. It helped me to keep off them, knowing how upset she had been.

I went with a guy called Shaun for a little while but I found out he was cheating on me so I dumped him.

When I was sixteen I met Dean. He was my second. I mean, I have messed around with lots of guys but I've only slept with two boys. I met Dean through his cousin by marriage, Sulman, who was a very good friend of mine. One night in the summer school holidays, Sul rang me and told me we were going for a drive and we were getting my friend Jenny as well. He said: "Dress up heaps nice, I've got someone who wants to meet ya."

So I sat in the car and saw this guy with long hair and earrings from base to apex and tattoos all over him and I didn't believe they were cousins, because Dean wasn't black. He had the shits anyway because Sul had said we were going to the club and of course Jenny and I weren't old enough to get into the club. Dean was eighteen.

The four of us drove around all night, just talking, and I was really hurt because Sul ended up getting with Jenny. We went to her house and I was sitting there thinking what a bastard Sul was. They went into the bedroom and I knew what they were doing and that was why Sul was with her and not with me – because she would put out and I wouldn't.

I started spilling my guts to Dean and telling him how much of a prick his cousin was and Dean then asked me what drugs I was on. I said: "*Pardon* me?" and he said: "Well, you're so skinny. Give us a look at your arms." I said: "I don't think so buddy"... it wasn't a real good start.

Anyway, I told him how I'd been sick and we ended up talking about it and then he leaned over and gave me a kiss on the cheek and said I shouldn't worry about it. He gave me a nice massage and then I sat on his lap and we started kissing. Then they took me home.

The next day I saw him but we didn't do anything. Then the next night he rang me up at about midnight. He was ringing from a club and he was pissed. He asked me out but he told me to think about it.

The next day, Dean came around and sat down and told Mum and Dad all about himself. He told them he had taken drugs and he had been in gaol. His uncle used to grow marijuana and he was sent out to sell it. So he was in a juvenile detention centre for a while.

Mum and Dad decided they didn't want me to see him. So the only way we could meet was through Sul.

I wanted so much to be with Dean. It just felt right. There was something about him that made me feel I would do anything for him.

Mum and Dad wouldn't change their minds and I was upset and angry. I threatened to move out of home. But I was depressed as well. I wouldn't normally have been like that. Mum rang Sul at work and asked him to come home and talk me out of leaving.

Anyway, I kept seeing Dean and pretending I was going places with Sul. It was two months before I slept with Dean. We were happy just having conversations. We talked about everything and anything. We have always talked. That is so important, to be able to talk to someone who cares about you. If you can't talk to the person, then it's not really a relationship.

One day, when I had said my girlfriend and Sul and I were going on a picnic, Mum packed us up a picnic lunch. She packed four of everything – four chicken legs, four sandwiches, four eggs, four plates, four sets of cutlery. She knew.

We finally had sex on the night of the picnic. We came home and Mum and Dad had gone out. It was incredibly romantic. He searched around my room for every candle that I owned and he lit every single one of them. We just started talking and kissing and touching and it all felt so right and it rolled into one big thing. It wasn't planned. We took off all our clothes and made love in the candlelight.

Mum rang in the middle of it and said she wanted to talk to Dean. I told her he wasn't there. She said: "I know you were with him today." He went home before they came back.

The next day Mum said she would rather we saw each other openly and not behind her back. Dean gets on well with my parents now and he has changed a lot. He mows the lawns, he does barbecues, he washes up. He comes over on Saturdays and we go out and on Sundays we stay home and do jobs. We even had a holiday together and my parents were fine about that. He has an apprenticeship now and he's had the same job for nearly a year which is the longest he has ever held down a job. He has given up drugs and is out of debt.

The relationship grew and grew. We used to be together in my room, watching television or listening to my stereo and we'd fall asleep and Mum and Dad would be waking us up so Dean could go to bed in the spare room. Finally one day they sat us down and asked us what we were going to do, whether we wanted to go on pretending we weren't sleeping together. We said we would prefer to sleep in the same bed and that was that. I was only sixteen but there wasn't a lot they could do to stop us and they knew that.

The magazines and everything say it's the experience that counts with sex – the more you do it the better it gets. Long before you get with any boy, you know what is supposed to happen from watching TV and reading.

I knew what we were doing was wrong, but it didn't bother me. I had always been a good girl and I didn't see how having sex with my boyfriend could make me a bad person.

I have one friend, Julia, who gets boyfriends easily because she's beautiful, but they never last longer than a couple of weeks because she won't give it up for them. Most boys will only wait four or five weeks maximum – if you won't sleep with them by then they don't want to have anything to do with you. Girls think beyond their pants, but boys don't.

Given my chances again, I'd prefer to be like Julia. But I used to be pretty stupid. With Dean, I was in love with the idea that I'd *got* someone and that he cared about me. I made sure first that he wanted me for more than just sex. Having Dean was a big thing for me.

Just before my seventeenth birthday I got pregnant. That *wasn't* supposed to happen. You don't read much about that in the magazines with the gorgeous girls on the front. I was supposed to be going on the pill. I actually had the pills there, waiting for my next period to start. But my next period never came. We only ever had unprotected sex once, and it was on the night of Dean's birthday. We were just lying in bed watching television and it just happened and we didn't bother with a condom.

Mum suspected it before I did, because I kept scratching my boobs. I was tired all the time and my periods stopped, but I'd had those symptoms when I was sick and I didn't believe I could be pregnant.

The first person I finally told was Dean and he couldn't believe it at first. He laughed, he thought I was joking. Then he said we had to sit down and talk about it.

He's like: "Well, I can start saving all my money and I can try to get overtime at work and we can work out what we need to buy ..."

I said: "Dean, I'm sixteen. I'm not married. I have no money. You only earn $100 a week." He said: "Don't you want to have it?" He was shocked. The thing is, he used to be a bit of a mattress-back and he'd had a child with another girl. Dean had tried real hard to stay in touch with her and he had spent a lot of money looking for her, but she went off to another state.

Eventually I told my doctor and we discussed the options. She was very good. She kept all my thoughts in perspective.

I definitely didn't consider adoption. If I was going to bring a kid into the world the child would be my responsibility and I would love it with all my heart. I wouldn't give it away.

The only two options for me were having the baby or having an abortion. I told my Mum and she started finding out about social security and pensions and she tried to work out how I could cope with school.

It seemed to me that everyone was making all these plans for me.

I wasn't bothered about the school stuff. I had been failing everything since I'd been sick. My main worry was hurting my parents and letting down their trust and loyalty. I knew it would be shameful for them to have to tell their friends. The way my parents looked at it was that I had so much ahead of me and if I had the baby I would be throwing all that away. My Mum told me to consider what I could offer a child. How would I support it? But she didn't tell me what to do. She let me make up my own mind.

I wanted to please the people around me and I wanted to keep my life the way it was. I'd already hurt my family –

having the baby would be like throwing everything they had done for me back in their faces.

One day my Mum said to me: "I'll get used to it. I'll get used to the sight of you walking down the street pushing a pram." I've never forgotten her saying that.

Anyways, I eventually decided to have the termination.'

Taking a break outside on the high verandah, Hannah lights a cigarette and watches the swaying carpet of trees. The mountain air is sharp and fresh. 'I love it here,' she says. She has stopped laughing. She finishes her cigarette – she's not allowed to smoke in the house – and returns to the scented lounge room to go doggedly on with her story.

'Mum went with me. I had the termination at a public hospital, and Medicare paid so it only cost $150.

Dean didn't ring me for a week beforehand. He said he would stand by any decision I made, but he also said how much he loved kids. He was very hurt. From when I told him about the pregnancy, he called it "our baby", or "shim", never "it". He wouldn't let me smoke. He kept putting his hand on my stomach and nagging me about what I was eating. He wondered what our baby would look like.

The place was awful, very clinical. They told me what they were going to do. I would rather not have known. I sat there for hours and girls were going in and walking out, crying. There was a fifteen-year-old girl there who was too far gone to have the operation – she was already on the table before they found out.

I had a local anaesthetic, but I could feel what they were doing. It's the most degrading position in the world, to be lying there with your legs in the air like that and all those people looking at you.

When I woke up it was dark outside.

Driving home I was in a lot of pain. It was like shocking period pain. And then there was this awful moment. My Mum was driving. Suddenly she said: "You know, I wanted you to keep that baby."

I started sobbing and crying. I said: "Why didn't you say? Why didn't you?"

"It's done now," she said.

I was full of regret after that. I wish I'd never done it. I never would again. It's the worst thing I've ever done.

This was something that was part of me and Dean. Not mine, ours. Of course it would only have been very small. Now that I'm studying all about babies, I know just how tiny my baby would have been.

Dean started ringing up but I wouldn't talk to him. I had the shits with him something fierce. He thought I blamed him but I didn't. I was angry because he should have been there, with me at the hospital. When I finally felt like speaking to him I just said: "Get around here and look after me." And he did.

I had two weeks off school.

That was two years ago. I like where I am with my life now, but I still think about that baby every day. What it would have looked like. What I would be doing with him or her right now. At night when I can't sleep I think: "Mmm, the cot would have gone there and I could have kept the nappies there..." It sort of gnaws at me. That's why I've decided to do early childhood for my career. I love kids. Only I know I will never have my own baby back.

In a way it bought Dean and me closer together. When you are talking about your baby, it's really personal. It's much more serious than anything you've talked about before. We did a lot of talking after that. Dean's attitude is: "Get on with your life and one day we'll have ten babies." But he was badly hurt by the whole thing.

It was more than a year before Dean and I slept together again. My parents won't let us share a bed any more – when he comes here, he sleeps alone.

We still find the time and place occasionally but we fool around more than we have intercourse. Being together is more important. I love him very much but if we couldn't talk to each other, the sex wouldn't happen.

My Mum was hurt too. She had so much trouble conceiving a child of her own, and then the only child she managed to have had a termination. One night they had a thing on abortion on the television and I got upset and ran into my room. Mum followed me. She told me I had to talk about it – it wasn't doing me any good bottling it all up. So I asked her what she would have done in my place and she said, real sadly: "I'd have kept it. But I'm not you."

Mum and Dad still do everything together. They went through a rough patch when the business was going bad but they hung in. I'd like Dean and me to be like them one day.'

'PLEASE HELP ME:
I'M DESPERATE AND I CAN'T
TELL MY MUM!'

According to the people who talk to them every day, kids don't know as much about sex as you might think.

Young people are much more aware of their sexuality than they were even one generation ago. However, for a lot of them, their bodies and feelings remain a mystery. Melissa Kang, an adolescent health specialist at the New Children's Hospital in Sydney, is also the resident doctor who advises readers of the national teenage magazine *Dolly*. Dr Kang receives seventy letters every month, almost all of them asking questions about normal adolescent sexual development.

According to Dr Kang, teenagers are very interested in their own physical and emotional state. 'Some of them know their bodies inside out – they are even concerned about their elbows. But when it comes to what they are doing with their bodies – such as what happens during sexual intercourse – they are surprisingly ignorant.'

As for the physical reality of pregnancy and childbirth (or conversely, the technicalities and moralities involved in abortion), unlike eager and curious prospective parents who have made a conscious decision to have children in their mid-twenties and beyond, teenage girls tend not to want to know. Even when the boys who have fathered their babies show curiosity, young women may see their interest as some kind of personal betrayal. Okay, so there's a baby growing in there ... but what about *her*?

Information, said Dr Kang, does not necessarily influence sexual behaviour. 'However, adolescents who have received a good sex education are much more likely to delay their sexual involvement.'

SHOULD IS HARD

Sex education *should* begin at home when children first become aware of themselves as sexual creatures. Their questions *should* be answered by their parents, in simple terms that they can understand. There is no need to worry about telling them too much. What young children don't understand they simply discard. Ideally, parents *should* continue to be their children's main source of information on sexuality.

Should is hard. *Should* is a word guaranteed to produce guilt.

As kids get older and as the questions become more difficult, requiring more explicit and personal replies, parents start deserting their posts in droves, leaving the dirty work to the foot soldiers in the form of their children's friends, or the platoon commanders who are, after all, trained teachers.

Schools are still very wary of what and how much information they *should* provide about sex. Education departments are afraid of a backlash from parents. Sex education is mandatory in most schools but teachers are left to their own devices about how to teach it and – surprise, surprise – many find it very difficult to discuss genitalia and intercourse with a classroom full of pubertally challenged adolescents. Not every teacher is as brave as Helen Garner, the brilliant Australian author and former school teacher who was sacked for providing her class with a graphic explanation of what was involved in oral sex. Not every student is as brave as the fourteen-year-old girl who put up her hand in class and asked whether a tampon would break her hymen. (It could, but she would still be a virgin.)

Most kids have trouble absorbing information about sexuality in a classroom situation. They can't equate the technical information with their own intense feelings and what is happening to their own bodies.

And anyway, a lot of them just don't listen.

FACTS AND FIGURES

There's a lot we take for granted. Too many adults tend to assume (wrongly) that all teenagers are 'doing it', and that this makes them promiscuous.

In early 1997 a team of researchers from the Centre for the Study of Sexually Transmissible Diseases at La Trobe University in Victoria carried out a national survey of sexual attitudes among students in Year Ten (fifteen and sixteen year olds) and Year Twelve (seventeen and eighteen year olds). More than 3550 students from 118 schools throughout Australia participated in the study, in which they were asked questions about HIV/AIDS and their own sexual health.

For the first time, the centre was able to establish changing sexual attitudes in adolescents, by comparing the 1997 results with a similar survey in 1992.

The survey found that 48% of Year Twelve students and 20% of Year Ten students have had sexual intercourse. Condom use had become widely accepted since 1992, with 54% of sexually active young people now using condoms at all times and 37% using condoms sometimes. There had also been a shift towards fewer sexual partners, with 16% of students having three or more sexual partners in the previous year compared with 22% in 1992.

Almost all of the students said they felt confident about insisting on the use of condoms and about saying no to unwanted sex.

Young women had fewer sexual partners in the last twelve months and were less likely to have casual sexual partners than young men. Year Twelve girls were more likely to have a steady sexual partner and to be using the contraceptive pill, even though the pill is no safeguard against sexually transmitted diseases (STDs). Young people in Year Ten generally had more sexual partners than the older students and were more likely to be having casual sex and to be using condoms. The Year Twelve girls were much more likely than the younger students to report feeling positive about their recent sexual experiences.

The bad news was that a quarter of the students admitted to having sex when they did not want to because they were drunk or high at the time. About 20% had not used condoms for the same reasons. More than 75% of the Year Ten students and 90% of Year Twelve students said they drank alcohol. Direct questions about marijuana were not asked.

The report revealed that students from rural towns, especially girls, were more likely to be sexually active than young urban dwellers.

While the awareness of HIV/AIDS was very high among all students, they were poorly informed about other STDs, such as gonorrhoea, syphilis and hepatitis. This is despite the fact that sexually active young Australians in the thirteen to nineteen age range are at high risk for STDs.

If 48% of students in their final year of high school are having sex, the best news from the study must be that more than half of them are not. Assuming that most of these young people are approaching their eighteenth birthdays, and remembering that previous generations of eighteen year olds probably had jobs and were frequently married at this age, the statistic is not quite so shocking.

That 20% of Year Ten students were having sex is of more concern. It's far from being a majority, but it's enough to worry parents, even if more of them are using condoms.

MAKING SENSE OF SEX

Shane Brown, coordinator of South Sydney Youth Services, is a youth worker and counsellor who has been working with young people for seventeen years. In 1996 he helped coordinate the Making Sense of Sex project during which more than 800 young people telephoned a specially trained panel of their peers to ask questions about sexuality.

'I think the trend to casual sex is changing, even among teenagers,' said Shane. 'We are returning to a situation where young people are less likely to indulge in casual relationships – at least less so now than five years ago. We are now entering a settling-down period where young people are questioning whether certain ways of behaving are right or not.

'I think the sexual revolution had a lot to do with why casual sex became more appealing to teenagers. But because there has been a growing perception that "everyone's doing it", casual sex is no longer shocking, it's no longer a way of making a statement against society.

'In the past two or three years there has been less pressure on girls to have casual sexual relationships. There is still a lot of pressure on boys to have sex as early as possible but I think that is changing too. Because young women are much more assertive, young men have to change. They have to respect and respond to the different ways young women are now approaching sexuality.

'Adolescent boys are finally catching on to the fact that *no* actually means *no*. Young women are much more able to articulate the *no*. They are also aware of potential pressure from boys – even from older guys to whom young teenage girls are often attracted.

'There is less stigma attached to girls being virgins than there used to be. The boys who come to our centre don't talk about the virginity issue any more – they've stopped saying that the most important thing they want in a girl is virginity.

'For girls this is a positive development, because it means that if she has had one sexual relationship (but has since reconsidered the pros and cons and put sex on the back burner for a while) there isn't the perception that she has ruined her reputation and her prospects of making good friends. In the past, too many girls were seen as sluts, and even thought of themselves that way, because they may have had more than one sexual partner.

'On the other hand, the girls are calling boys who sleep around "sluts".

'Parents and educators are not working together effectively to educate today's adolescents about sex and sexuality. Right now there is an "us against them" mentality, with resentment on both sides. There is no clear agreement on how sex education should be achieved.

'Educators need to be much more responsive to what parents want. They need to talk to parents and parents need to talk to them. The reason why so many educators are going directly to the young people is because sometimes it's hard to get those parents on board.

'Parents should be asking their kids what they are doing and why. Ask them to think about what they are doing and whether it is the right thing. Debate. Discuss. Don't fight. Talk.'

WHY DO THEY DO IT? WHY NOT?

The Youth Team at Family Planning NSW regularly conducts education sessions in schools. The following comments were made on 'graffiti sheets' during programs designed to draw out young people's ideas, values and attitudes to sexuality.

WHY GIRLS HAVE SEX	WHY GIRLS DON'T HAVE SEX
Wanted to know what it was like	Not emotionally ready
In love	Don't believe in sex before marriage
For pleasure	Not educated about it
For fun	Religious reasons
To keep my boyfriend	Bad experience with it
They're sluts	Fear of pregnancy
To piss parents off	Not interested
Forced	Pressure from parents
They're prostitutes	Abused as a child
Fear	Too young
Something to talk about	Scared of STDs
Boyfriend wants it	Feel uncomfortable about it
New experience	Too sensible
Romance	No partner
Excitement	Scared of AIDS
Curiosity	Why give guys the satisfaction?
Peer pressure	Risk your reputation
To get pregnant	Not mature enough
To get popular	Don't like boyfriend enough
Because I was drunk	Scared it will hurt
Raped	To be an individual
	Don't want to
	Everybody else does
	I'm strong enough to say no.

WHY BOYS HAVE SEX	WHY BOYS DON'T HAVE SEX
Horny	Scared
Peer pressure	Worried about catching and transmitting diseases
Want to experience what it's like	Don't want to
Experimental purposes	Not ready
Desperate	Can't get it up
Wanna be cool	Worried about getting a girl pregnant
For pleasure	Unsure of sexuality
For fun	Embarrassed
To feel manly and mature	Don't know how
Curiosity	Can't get a date
Pissed	Scared I won't satisfy
To have something to talk about to friends	Against my religion

Ben sat on a kitchen stool, his huge feet wound around the wooden legs, and watched his mother unpack groceries. Di was a bustling, busy, talkative person. She didn't have a paid job like most of his mates' mothers. She called herself an at-home Mum, but in reality she was rarely at home. She was involved in heaps of things and she spent a great deal of time charging about and talking to people and everyone knew who she was.

They knew who he was too. It wasn't just because of his mum. He and his brothers played a lot of sport. Ben wasn't brilliant, not Aussie rep. material, like Luke and Sam, but he was pretty damn good, all the same.

Ben wasn't sure whether he liked being in a family that was talked about. The thing about Lucy was that nobody seemed to know her. You never saw her parents, you never heard about her. She'd come to the school two years ago and all he knew was that her parents were divorced, she was from somewhere 'up north', her skin was as pale as cream and she held herself very straight, in a single graceful line from her small feet to her pale, silky hair. He didn't know whether she had sisters or brothers, like him. He didn't know where she lived. He did know that she had a wonderful smile and when they read funny bits in the books and plays they talked about in English, she laughed at the same parts as him. She had a deep, gutsy laugh. It was a surprise the first time he heard it. He had expected it to be light and lilting, like the way she walked.

His mother was asking him something. What? She was thanking him for helping her unpack. Except he hadn't. Sarcasm is the lowest form of wit, he told her. She came over to the bench and sat down, resting her chin in her hands.

'What's the matter with you lately, Ben?' she said.

He scowled at her and hopped off the stool. 'Nothing,' he said.

'Okay,' she said slowly. 'But is it a girl? Do you have a girl problem?'

He was going to ignore her and walk away but he hesitated. They had always talked. For as long as he could remember, his mother, as annoying as she was in many ways, had always been happy to answer his questions. Until recently, he had been happy to answer hers. Not that she asked a lot. He had to give her that.

He came back to the bench and sat down. 'Her name's Lucy,' he said. 'I really like her. We've hardly talked.'

'Why not?'

'What would people say? What about the guys? And her friends? She's always in the middle of a great crowd of females.'

'So she's not one of these eager little things who keep ringing you up in the evenings?'

Ben looked scornful. 'Of course not. She wouldn't do that. They're just friends, anyway. Lucy's different.'

'How?' asked his mother.

Ben sighed. 'She makes me want to ...' He stopped and blushed. 'I dunno.'

Di looked down and traced a pattern on the bench top. 'If you really like her,' she said slowly, 'I don't see how it matters what other people say – her friends or yours.'

Ben shrugged. How could he tell his mother that his friends would find it all a huge joke. That they would talk about it and tease him about it and before long it would be all about how far he was getting. It would end up being all about sex. That was all his friends talked about lately, if the subject was girls. Sex. Well, sex and soccer.

'Why don't you ask her to go somewhere with you, so you can talk without all the others listening and watching you?'

'God, Mum, look at me!' Ben yelled. The 'me' came out in a squeak, even though he thought he'd finished with the whole voice change bit. He ripped off his cap and shoved his face forward, close to hers. 'My forehead's like a pizza, my hands are as big as family pies, my feet are like trucks, I can't walk properly, I can't talk properly...'

He stood up again and kicked aside the stool and rammed his hat on his head. When he looked at his mother again, she was smiling.

'I'm glad you think it's funny,' he growled.

Di came around the bench and looked up at him, still smiling. 'You've got so tall and gorgeous,' she said softly. 'She'd better start noticing you soon or the other girls will beat her to the punch.'

'You're just saying that because you're my mum,' he muttered as he walked out of the kitchen.

But he felt a bit better.

JAKE'S STORY

He is thin but he has the long, taut and sinewy limbs of a disciplined dancer. He has a narrow face and high cheekbones, small, light-coloured eyes, thin fair curly hair, cut short and combed neatly back, translucent skin, tanned pale brown by the summer sun that he's missed so much. He's been away but he's glad to be back, living in the family's beautifully restored Federation home. Reclining gracefully on the deep leather couch, he is more elegant than many girls; hesitant about beginning but confident about what he's going to say, he asks permission to smoke.

Jake is the eldest son of a career couple whose serious and committed concerns about children's health and safety and environmental issues are complemented by exceptionally liberated views on lifestyle and morality. Jake is twenty.

'We were brought up knowing we could do anything – anything we liked. If we wanted to try something, like play an instrument, or play a particular sport, or see certain friends, our parents bought us what we needed and organised the lessons or coaching or transport – they made everything possible. I don't know why that was, but whatever we wanted to do, we could. Nothing was a problem.

My parents run their own company and work very long hours, but they've been successful so we have enjoyed a pretty good life.

My Mum had a restricted childhood – she had to put herself through university for ten years – so it's mainly been

Mum who makes it all happen for us and actually encourages us. She's the pants wearer, she wanted it to be easier for us. She pushed the music, she wouldn't let me give up the saxophone or dancing – which I'm grateful for now.

I was encouraged but not forced to study. I went to a small private school where the teachers really cared about us. My friends and I were the cream – we were the band, we were the music gurus. Towards the end of Year Twelve I went to the state library to do my studying. I did reasonably well, although I wasn't highly motivated.

When I left school I enrolled at a dance course and I moved out of home for a while and got a job as a waiter to get some money. I went to London for a year after getting accepted into a dance school there. Before I came home again I went to Italy and I spent a month travelling in Europe. Now I'm back home again, working at the same restaurant where I was before and starting all over again.

I've been a bit rebellious I suppose; I've been difficult, but I'm pleased that I've had such an unrestricted childhood. We were always allowed to find things out for ourselves. I was never blocked by my parents' opinions on things.

The first sexual experience I remember having was when I was in Year Three. I would have been eight and we went to this place to be minded every day after school. My trouble buddy was Greg Watson and we were always in strife. We started looking at girlie pictures in magazines. I remember being invited to the vacant lot next door to watch Greg and his sister do this thing together. I didn't participate, but I can still remember it, I can see them. He would have been about nine and she was a couple of years older. They used this rude word a lot while they were at it. I remember being frightened, but they didn't get caught. We just went back into the centre afterwards, and started playing in the sand pit.

I went home and asked Mum and Dad what "fuck" meant and they told me it was a swear word for something you did with a female. I don't think that's when they sat down and told me where babies came from. That came a bit later, when I was nine and my parents used that book, *Where Did I Come From,* with the sperm wearing the top hat.

Not long after that I started playing with Mat and Debbie who lived next door. Mat and I played around once or twice. We tried lying on top of each other and taking it in turns to be the girl. We just kissed and cuddled, but there was no climax or ejaculation – I suppose we were too young. When Debbie played we took our clothes off and tried to experiment. We tried to have sex, mainly because it was a naughty thing to do. We were in our bedrooms after school – their parents were never in the house at that time. We decided to flip a coin and if it came down as heads we were allowed to kiss and if it was tails we would have sex. It came down as heads. So we flipped it over.

Debbie was a bit older – about twelve I suppose. We tried to have sex standing up. She was taller than me so I stood on a chair, but that didn't work. Then we tried various positions on the floor but that didn't work either. Her hips hadn't spread – it was impossible, really. We did this twice, once after school and once when they were sleeping over and we all slept in the same room. I think mainly we were just curious. I wonder if everybody did stuff like that when they were little?

We moved just after that and I missed this girl called Amber who lived down the road and I wrote her a letter and asked her to come and visit and stay the night. She did, and my parents let us sleep in the same room and there was a lot of cuddling and kissing in my bed, but that was all. I asked her if she had had sex yet and she said she didn't think so, but I didn't really care. It was the cuddling I liked. We would have been about ten I suppose.

By Year Six it had stopped being a kid's game and had become more serious. Being in love was a big issue – love letters in class and all that. I started at the private school that year and there was this lovely girl, Daniela – I was besotted with her. I wrote her so many letters, but all we ever did was go behind the bushes in the playground and kiss once, on the lips. That was all that ever happened. I was writing her letters mostly – "Why do you like Tim and not me? Why did you give him that bag of twisties?" Really romantic stuff. Then she broke it off and I remember bursting into tears in the park and crying and crying and crying.

Year Seven was a very school-oriented year. In Year Eight I made a very good friend called Johan. That was the year we tried smoking, we tried drinking, we tried marijuana. I fell in love with Sarah, a girl I met at camp. We went on a date when we got back and I had my first proper kiss with her. I was so shocked. I walked out of the movie theatre and went into the toilet and just stood there for ages, staring at myself in the mirror and spinning out about the whole thing.

Until then we had all just been playing games, copying adults, pushing bodies together, pressing lips against lips. Kissing Sarah was the first genuine sexual experience I had. It was more than just lips, it was everything.

I called her every night for six weeks. I was totally in love. But we only met one more time. I went to meet her at her school dance but I wasn't allowed in because I didn't go to her school. We sat in the park and waited for my parents to come and collect me at the end of the evening and we kissed and talked. It was great. It was wonderful.

We broke up after that because I was double-dating – in other words I was seeing Marnie, from my school.

Of course I told Johan everything. I told him how I'd kissed Sarah and put my hand on her breast – stuff like that. About that time I also asked another mate about masturbation and whether anything happened when he did it. He said it did and I was wondering why it wasn't happening for me. At the end of Year Eight, when I was about fourteen, it did.

I knew I could have asked my parents about masturbation, but my friends have always been a very central part of my life. I have always known I could ask my parents anything. But just the thrill of talking about it with friends makes it more exciting. And I was curious about what was happening to them as well.

From Year Nine, when we were fifteen, there was this little group of about six of us, both boys and girls. It was an incestuous little circle – we'd all hop around and say we loved this person and then it would be that person, but it was always within the same group of people.

We didn't actually "go out". We went to each other's places and watched videos or got drunk or smoked dope. Mostly one of us got marijuana from school or sometimes our parents had some – it always lasted for ages. The alcohol belonged to our families. When we were drunk or high we would crash out in couples and we would masturbate each other, although we didn't always need to be on drugs to do it.

It was like – one night with Marnie, for example – we were lying head to head at an angle, and we touched and stroked each other until we reached orgasm. We didn't take our clothes off, it was just stroking under the clothes. It wasn't just the sex. It was the company. In my group, friendship came first. Friendship was more important than sexual experimentation. When there was bickering and trouble, sorting it out was more important to us than the sex stuff. On the other hand, the touching and cuddling brought us all closer together.

Swapping around didn't cause any trouble, at least not between the guys. Anyway, with me it was always only either me and Marnie or me and Emily.

At the end of Year Ten, when we were all turning sixteen, there was a big split with the group. Two of them became a regular couple and my friendship with Johan finished and I made friends with Jimmy and Ria. About that time, the school certificate exams were over and school and the people from school stopped meaning much to me and drinking and stuff became more important. At the end of that year I finally had sex.

It was the beginning of the summer holidays. I spent eight weeks constantly with Jimmy and Ria: a night at his house, a night at mine, a night at hers. We went everywhere together – playing pool, getting drunk, having curry for lunch – we went to places all over the city and we tried to pretend we were more cultured and sophisticated than we really were.

Ria came over to my house one afternoon and we got stoned and we both felt very horny. So we walked down the hall to the cupboard where the condoms were kept. My parents had always made sure my brothers and I all knew there were condoms in the house and that they were for our use. So Ria and I helped ourselves to some condoms and then we went outside and we walked up the backyard to the shed, of all places, and we hugged and kissed and took our clothes off. She was a tiny, skinny little thing. She was a tomboy sort of girl. We were in love with each other as friends. We were very straight with each other from the start, about how we felt. I knew she was in love with Jimmy as well as me.

For my first time it was very interesting. We did it standing up. Because she was so small she had to stand on a bale of hay that was there for the guinea pigs. We sort of knew what to do. It was very frank and open – I knew I had to put a condom on. I'm so glad we were friends first. There were no hang ups about anything. I'm so pleased it was Ria.

Every few weeks after that, whenever we were drunk or stoned, and we were on our own, we had sex. Jimmy and Ria didn't have sex and when the three of us were together we were still going out and trying new things. Ria lived right in the city and her mother worked nights so she was never there. We often slept there, but my parents always knew where I was. I started sleeping in the days and spending most of the nights out.

It was never established that Ria and I were boyfriend and girlfriend. We were always just friends except on one occasion when there were a lot of us at a party and Marnie was there and I still loved Marnie and I wanted to spend time with her that night. And Ria got really upset – because she loved me, I think, and she was crying and had to be consoled by her female friends. I pleaded ignorance of what was wrong, of course.

For the next two years, I suppose I was having a relationship with Ria. We were at different schools but we'd spend most weekends together and every couple of weekends, if there were just the two of us, we'd have sex. It was never planned in any way. We'd just be out – playing pool together, looking for dope together. Then we'd go back to her place. It was very free. We tried various positions. We did it in the kitchen, all over her house, really. Her mother just wasn't there and the flat was near all the cool places so we could do whatever we felt like and we really enjoyed ourselves. We both started working in restaurants about that time, although I was doing my HSC.

School started getting really important again in Year Twelve and I saw less of Jimmy and Ria but after I left school and went to dance school I made a lot of new friends. I met a guy called Will who became – and still is – my very closest friend in the whole world.

On the last day of school, Ria burst into tears and told me she thought she might be a lesbian so that was the end of our sexual relationship.

The first term of dance school was awkward. I didn't like it much, with everything being so different. It was also the first time I really saw the gay scene.

Will was a redneck from Queensland who suddenly decided at the end of the first term that he was gay. He talked to me about it and that brought up questions for me. It was just curiosity at first. I think everybody asks the question of themselves sooner or later – everybody wonders at least once what it's like to kiss another guy.

Having a gay friend made me think about it. But Will decided he was, in fact, in love with me. There was a lot of sexual tension in the air after that, and I suppose I enjoyed the attention he was giving me. We went away to his parents' beach house and we were sleeping in the same bed together and he put his hand down between my legs and touched me. I said I wasn't interested. It made things difficult, especially for him. He didn't give up the idea of us being together until a year after that, not until just before I went to London. We had lots of huge arguments about things but it always came back to sex in the end.

I had a relationship with a girl called Ailsa for about three months. I was deeply in love with her and I slept with her, but she didn't love me. As soon as I broke it off with her, she decided she loved me after all. It was one of those things, but I didn't go back to her. Instead, a few months later, I went to a party with a friend of mine, who was gay. His name was Laurence and he was my hairdresser. I suppose he was attractive – I didn't think about it – he was just my hairdresser. He was about fifteen years older than me – I was about eighteen at the time – and I thought he was very groovy.

We were on the dance floor at about 3 am when he kissed me. It was the first time I had ever kissed another guy. For me it was an experiment. It was purely sexual. I had taken ecstasy. I suppose the drug broke down my inhibitions. I thought: "Oh, he's kissing me."

I've always been open-minded about the whole gay thing. Do what you want to do, be what you want to be, that's how we were brought up. As I wasn't going out with any girl at the time I didn't see anything wrong with it.

I didn't do anything to instigate it. Laurence did everything. I admit it was in my mind, the idea of it. I had talked about it to Ria and Jimmy. I knew it would be a one night stand.

We went back to his place and we slept together but we didn't have intercourse. We just kissed and played with each other.

I still don't know if I enjoyed it or not. Or why I did it. Afterwards I just got up and left, which made him feel bad. He didn't know it was my first time. He was really shocked when I told him. You see, unfortunately for me, because of the way I dress and the fact that I hang out in the eastern suburbs, I come across to a lot of people as being gay.

But the point is, it was a gay dance party and I had taken ecstasy. It was his domain, so to speak, and I should have known better. I get cross with straight people, because they go to gay parties and then get all horrified and affronted when they get their arses squeezed.

I left and went home and went for a walk and thought about it, and I thought about telling my parents and I thought: "Am I gay now?" Every question that came into my mind was a cliché.

I wondered what life would be like as a gay man. I wondered about whether it really mattered whether I was straight or gay or if I was attracted to both sexes, or to none. I thought about AIDS but I had known about that for years and I thought that as long as I was safe and careful I could prevent it.

I was pretty moody for about two weeks and I didn't tell anyone at first but then I told Will. That was a big mistake of course. The problem with Will is that I have always considered him to be my closest friend but he thinks of me as a potential sexual partner.

What I did with Laurence I could never have done with Will. He was my best friend. All the time we had been friends I had maintained this strict rule – that we would never be sexual together. It wasn't what I wanted. I knew it would be wrong. I knew if we did anything like that it would be the end of our friendship, that it would change things between us. I don't know how I knew, but I knew. I know.

He was very upset. It made him angry that I hadn't had my first gay experience with him. We had fights and arguments for a long time. It kept coming up and it made me angry because I had always made it quite clear that I didn't want a gay relationship with him.

I never considered myself to be truly gay. I thought of it as an isolated incident, an experiment which was mainly because I was taking drugs. A lot of people take ecstasy to get rid of their inhibitions, to make it easier to have sex. I am sure that if I hadn't gone to that party and taken ecstasy I would never have gone with Laurence.

At the end of my first year a girl from my dance class finally made it clear that she liked me. This turned out to be my first long-term relationship with a girl. Shar and I were together for over a year. She made all the initial moves, sat in my lap, made it known she was interested in me. I asked her back to my house and we went out for about three or four weeks before we had sex. I didn't even raise the question. I was happy the way things were, just kissing and cuddling. Then one night she said: "Shall we have sex?" It wasn't very romantic. It never is.

Things improved when she went on the pill. Uninhibited sex is a lot more enjoyable. I had never had sex without a condom before – oh except one night with Ria when we were stupid – we rushed out and bought the morning-after pill the next day.

When I went to London, Shar said she might meet me over there. She took the whole relationship more seriously than I did. I really thought it would all just fall apart while we were apart but she wrote to me regularly and I really needed those letters when I was feeling a bit isolated. She eventually came to London and we lived together for two months, in the flat I was sharing with a gay guy called Dino and another girl.

I started questioning everything I was doing that year – I was studying dance six days a week and I was very tired. But I loved Dino's company and I loved the way he lived. I tried to discuss my sexuality with Shar, but she didn't understand. She moved out.

I had started talking to a psychiatrist at the dance school about the possibility that I might be gay. I was thinking about it a lot.

Shortly after Shar moved out, Dino and I were dancing at a club and, again under the influence of ecstasy, Dino and I started kissing. We kissed and kissed and we hugged a lot and eventually we went home and slept together. We had oral sex but I didn't ejaculate. So I decided I was definitely going to come out as a gay man. I would wear the clothes, I would live the life.

The trouble is, two nights later I tried the kissing and touching and oral sex again, without drugs, and I realised I didn't really like it at all.

I've never liked having sex with people just for the sex. I prefer to be in love with the person. I've had a couple of one night stands with girls, usually when I've been drunk, but I don't like the idea of just having a root. When you're in love, when the person really means something to you, you get so much more enjoyment out of sex. You can give them more pleasure. With Ria, whom I loved for so long, it was always understood that we were friends more than lovers.

I had to admit to Dino that I really enjoyed being his friend but I didn't want to be his lover. It was very hard for me to tell him and he was upset but he was cool. He didn't make me feel bad about it.

One afternoon I was talking about this to the accountant at the dance school who was gay. He invited me to his flat to talk some more and he and his boyfriend ... well, "took advantage of me" is probably the best way to describe it. We had a few drinks and then he took me upstairs and started kissing me. I had sex with him and his partner.'

For the first time, Jake is visibly upset. Not for the first time, he looks very young. He blinks rapidly several times, sighs, lights another cigarette and with small, neat furrows knotting on his forehead, he continues.

'I have no idea why I did that. I didn't enjoy it. Mind you, I did finally ejaculate. But there was no kissing, nothing nice. It was just sex. I found out later they did it to two other boys at the school who were also confused about their sexuality.

I haven't resolved the question of my sexuality. I consider myself someone who sleeps with men and women – what is important to me is that I love them.

I went home and told Dino. He invited me to go for a holiday to Italy to meet his family. This was the end of my time at the dance school so I worked in a bar to save enough money and I went to stay with Dino. We slept together on one occasion, when we were at the beach and we were very drunk. It was all really lovely and romantic and I knew where the events of the day were heading. We tried anal sex but I didn't like it. It hurt. Another day we were in the shower and Dino came in and gave me oral sex. We were rushed for time so I returned the favour. But after that I backed off. I felt guilty about stuffing Dino around.

When I arrived back in London, Shar was back there too so we started seeing each other again. We slept together twice, mainly because neither of us had a boyfriend at the time. She was shocked about what I'd been doing but she came to terms with it.

I decided to come home. I've been very lucky with my parents. When I went to England my father said to me: "When you go to a new country, who you are is all you have. It makes you think a great deal about your life, it makes you question everything you do." The whole time I was questioning my sexuality I was able to talk about it on the phone to my mother.

I have never felt that what I've done with people is morally wrong. I've always tried to do what I think is right, not what other people think is right. I don't agree with any religious teaching on the subject. But loving someone is more important to me than having sex.

I've always thought I would marry one day and have children and a house – the gay thing has jeopardised that in a way.

I've been back in Australia for about six months and I've been celibate all that time. Will is still my best friend. He has a boyfriend now and sometimes I get a bit jealous – but I would feel just the same if he was spending time with a steady girlfriend. There will never be anything sexual between us.

I feel very frustrated. I'd love to meet a female partner who I could love but who would also be my mate, the way Dino was. I haven't had that sort of relationship with a girl.

My parents live and work together. They are together twenty-four hours a day, seven days a week and they have been like that for twenty-five years. And they are still in love with each other. I find that so admirable. That's what I want. That's what I would like more than anything in the world.'

In the end he was spared the embarrassment of asking her out. He had been to the movies with Tom and Ritchie and he saw her coming out. She was with Rebecca, a chunky little girl he had known since kindergarten. Taking a big breath and not letting himself think about it, he went straight over and said hi.

'What are you two going to do now?' he asked Rebecca, but he was looking at Lucy. She wasn't smiling, but she was looking right back. 'We thought we might go and get a drink and a meal,' he said smoothly. 'We did?' said Ritchie, looking startled. But Ben was on a roll. He kept on looking at Lucy. 'Want to come?'

The girls looked at each other. The secret messages that girls send bounced from eyeball to eyeball and Rebecca turned and grinned at the three boys. 'Where'll we go?' she asked.

It had to be the golden arches, as none of them had much money. After his incredibly suave performance in the cinema foyer, Ben ran out of revs, but luckily Ritchie was the sort of guy who wouldn't stop talking under water. They discussed movies, and the stars they most liked and those they hated. Then Lucy made a comment about Australian movies, and how they never had storyline like American films.

'They just sort of start and go along for a while, and then there are some nude scenes and a whole lot of sweaty sort of love scenes, and then the movie goes on for a while and ends,' she said.

There was a silence while they all thought about what she'd said. Tom had punched Ritchie when she said 'sweaty sort of love scenes' and Ben pretended not to notice, but he wondered how he could call such immature clowns his friends. Lucy started to go pink. 'Well that's what I think anyway.'

'No, hang on,' said Ritchie. 'What about *Strictly Ballroom*? That had a climax.' Everyone started talking at once. Ben kept quiet. He thought how fantastic this girl was, so quietly confident, yet she could get a whole group of people talking about something really interesting. He looked at her. When she smiled he saw her wonderfully even white little teeth. He finally let himself believe, from the faint flush on Lucy's smooth cheek, from the way she looked directly at him when she spoke, that she liked him.

It was lovely, just sitting there, looking at her, knowing he could talk to her if he wanted to and she would answer. The hard part, the wishing and the hoping and the dreaming, was over. From now on, everything would be easy.

He was wrong.

LOVE OR SEX? GREAT EXPECTATIONS

(A CHAPTER MAINLY FOR KIDS)

Sex is mysterious. Sex is outrageous. Sex is beautiful. Sex is dirty. Sex is natural. Sex is shocking. Sex is good. Sex is bad – unless it is reduced to a meaningless recreational activity, in which case there is no way of determining whether it's good or bad or not. Sex is exciting – unless you have a persistent partner, a headache or some very small children. In any of these cases, sex might sometimes be less exciting than the prospect of a good night's sleep. Sex is fulfilling. Sex is frustrating. Sex is for everyone – unless you are too young, too old, too sick, too healthy (in training!), too good or too bad.

Confused? That's sex for you.

Love and sex and feelings have been confusing young men and women since before we began counting centuries. The rules on sex may be more relaxed than they used to be, but falling in love has never changed. The big problem these days is that a lot of young people get the two things mixed up.

There is no such thing as only one true love for each person in the world. You can fall in love many times, with different people. Of course, the ideal for most people is to end up with one person whom they will love truly and forever for the rest of their life.

GOOD LOVE OR BAD LOVE?

Professor Sol Gordon is a well-known American psychologist, sex educator and author who has spent nearly half a century talking to kids about love and sex. In Australia recently, Professor Gordon shared his wisdom and experience with educators and school students who were enlightened, delighted – and rather relieved – to hear what he had to say. Most of the ideas in this section are based on his research.

If you think you're in love, you probably are. But there are two kinds of love – mature love, which is good for you, and immature love, which is bad. How do you tell the difference between them? At first it's impossible, because the initial symptoms are the same.

After a few months, once you've really got to know the person, the differences become obvious. Good love makes you a nicer person. It gives you energy, it makes you want to be kind to people. When you are experiencing good love, you are a nice person to be with and you even help out at home without being asked. Your parents look at you with startled smiles. Good love makes you happy most of the time.

Bad love is exhausting and it makes you mean. It wears you out, it takes away your incentive to do anything for yourself, it makes you inconsiderate and obsessed with your own feelings. You can't be expected to wash the car or make your bed. You're in love and your family raises eyes to the ceiling and counts the days until you are out of it again.

Young people often fail to realise that it takes several months to get to know someone really well. First comes friendship. Then comes intimacy. Then, perhaps, comes love. Sex, if it happens, needs to be a long way down the program of events because when it happens it has the potential to change not only the relationship, but both the young people involved.

Good love involves communication and understanding between the girl and the boy. An enjoyable and fulfilling relationship which makes both people happy is based on friendship, caring about each other's welfare and interests, trusting each other and sharing a sense of humour. Being able to laugh together is a very important part of love.

Violence – hurting each other in any way at all – is never a sign of love.

If a young couple believe they love each other and eventually decide to have sex together, they should be prepared for the reality – which is usually very different from what they've seen on the screen. Sex is not something wonderful that just happens. Like most potentially wonderful experiences, it gets better as the two people involved learn more about each other.

They should also use condoms – the first time and every time afterwards. Unfortunately, too many girls think practical preparation, like having condoms handy, is unromantic. Too many boys think it's not their problem.

Many young people are virgins and have made the decision to remain so until marriage or at least until they are older and in a committed relationship. The sexual revolution has changed things so much these days that it is often these young men and women, rather than those who are having sex from an early age, who worry about whether they are normal.

Of course they are normal. There is nothing wrong and everything right about making the decision to have sex only with the person you have sworn to love for life. However, virgins should not expect multiple orgasms on their wedding night. For them, as for everyone, good sex goes with good loving and takes time.

It is a fact that even adults who love each other very deeply may not enjoy a satisfactory sexual relationship. The reasons for this can be medical, social or psychological and may be traced right back to their adolescence – they are frequently related to unsatisfactory sex in their teenage years. Solving problems related to sexuality involves time, communication and a great deal of patience, elements that are not generally in good supply among adolescents. Sex problems are simply something you don't need or want to be worrying about when you are inundated with all the other concerns involved in growing up.

Sex education, both at home and at school, starts with loving parents and caring teachers. Young people who are given the confidence in themselves to make the right decision at the right time, who can say no if they want to, who can insist on condom use if they say yes, and who love and respect themselves as well as others – these are the kids who pass sex education with flying colours.

Some young people have been hurt by the worst kind of sex education. Professor Gordon has a special message for abused adolescents:

'No matter what has happened to you as a child – no matter how bad it was – that doesn't mean you have to be "damaged" for the rest of your life. If you put most of your energy into blaming others for your troubles, you won't make it as a responsible mature adult. The best revenge you can take on those who have hurt you is to live your life well.'

In the long term, the most important ingredients in marriage are neither love nor sex – they are friendship and a sense of humour. Marriage is not what most kids are concerned about, but it's something to remember in the future.

LOVE OR SEX?

Young lovers run the very serious risk of confusing sex with love.

'We're in love so it's okay to do what we want,' they say. But an awful lot of the time they are not in love with each other at all. The girls are in love with the idea of love and the boys are in love with the idea of sex and getting the chance to do it with a girl.

Which means it's not okay at all.

In their early teenage years, adolescents are totally absorbed in themselves – their feelings, their bodies, their social lives and their friends – but their friendships are based more on how they feel about others than about how others feel. They have great difficulty understanding their own emotions, let alone other people's. Being in love is a wonderful feeling but if the love is returned, it also makes us hugely responsible for the other person's feelings.

Boys, whose testosterone is pumping powerfully through their bodies as they race through puberty, may sincerely believe that girls are being equally driven by the same sort of sexual urges. This is not often the case, although the girls who have watched a lot of love scenes on the television are probably pretty good at pretending otherwise. In truth, the things that encourage teenage girls to have sex are more to do with power and peer pressure than with love or intimacy or sexual urge. Even girls who don't particularly want to be bothered with boys admit that it's terribly important to be seen by their friends as having a boyfriend; once they've managed it, they worry about losing him. So ...

Because young men are not very good at sexual intercourse and generally ejaculate (come) very quickly, the girls are often left low and dry and wondering what happened, or whether it happened at all, or why it hurt so much. But the boys are confused too. They are under pressure to get rid of their virginity; they are worried about being seen as homosexual if they don't. Many believe sex is what girls expect.

By confusing sex with love, young people can and often do develop an inability to enjoy a healthy, long-term relationship. Even as they grow older, they flit from one person to another in their quest for what they think is 'love' but turns out to be sex – and as good as sex can be, it's no substitute for genuine love and true intimacy. At best, this inability to form a commitment leads to immense hurt, loneliness and vulnerability. At worst, young people may find themselves with partners as immature as they are, in an unstable, violent and unhappy situation, where rage, abuse and often alcohol and drugs are used as a substitute for their frustration and lack of satisfaction.

WHAT DOES BEING IN A SEXUAL RELATIONSHIP INVOLVE?

When girls and boys become close friends they form a relationship. In some ways it is the same as the relationship they have with their parents, sisters and brothers or same sex friends. They care about each other. They are interested in the same things. They want to make each other happy. They want to be together.

Friendship should not come at a cost to your own personal space. Friends usually become physically and emotionally close to you, but it is up to you to decide how close you allow them to come. Building a really good friendship takes quite a long time.

Sometimes, when boys and girls spend a lot of time together and are utterly happy in each other's company, they become more than friends – they fall in love.

It is absolutely possible for two young people to have a loving relationship without having sex.

The best thing about being young and in love is that the simple pleasures of life become more enjoyable. Yet many boys and girls in steady relationships are frustrated by the lack of things to do. Sometimes boredom leads to sex, even if it hasn't been planned. Lying around, talking, looking, touching – one thing can lead to another.

Love is a beautiful thing. It's a terrific and wonderful feeling and should be enjoyed. However, at a practical level, love leads to a lot of complications and one of them is sexual desire. Pounding hearts and thrilling emotions send messages to the brain which then signals the body to get physical. These messages are pretty hard to ignore.

Young people generally believe that if they are not having sexual intercourse, they are not in a sexual relationship. Actually, any sort of sexual contact makes the relationship a sexual one. Sexual contact means giving each other physical and emotional pleasure. It is quite different to the hand shakes, the hugs and the linked arms of platonic friends. For adolescents, compromise is safer and often more enjoyable than going all the way.

The decision to have sexual intercourse is a very important one. If two young people decide to go ahead, they must be absolutely certain that this is what they *both* want. Then there are a lot of questions each of them should ask themselves:

- Do I feel old enough and responsible enough to be doing this?
- Am I doing this for me or for him/her?
- Am I prepared to use a condom?
- If something goes wrong and we make a baby, am I prepared for that responsibility?
- Am I just trying to prove something to myself or him/her?
- How will I feel about him/her afterwards?
- How will I feel about myself?

Sex changes the dynamics of the relationship. The boy and girl are no longer just together. They are lovers.

Being in a sexual relationship means being faithful to your partner. The majority of young people want monogamous relationships. All of them without exception are very hurt when their steady girlfriend or boyfriend cheats on them.

Being in a committed relationship brings a great deal of pleasure and can double your fun. Having sex in a relationship makes things more complicated. There's fighting, for example. Few couples agree about everything. Disagreements can easily turn into hurtful and insulting comments, unnecessary criticism, sarcasm and sulking – even physical attacks. Sex leaves young people open to greater hurt.

Spending time together is an important part of a steady sexual relationship. You have to be prepared to plan ahead;

you might have to sacrifice doing something you really like doing in order to spend more time with the person you love.

A lot of boys grumble that since their mate found himself a steady girlfriend, he's missing out on a lot of fun with the blokes. This is true – but he's made his choice. However, people who keep their friends, and keep up with their own interests, their sport, music and studies, are more likely to remain interesting to their boyfriend or girlfriend than those who allow their lives to revolve entirely around one person.

Other things can go wrong with a sexual relationship. Jealousy raises its nasty head. Sometimes you lose other friends. After a while you may find out there's something about your lover that you really don't like at all. Does it have to mean the relationship is over, or can you learn to accept this difficulty while continuing to love the person despite his or her faults, rather than because of them?

When problems can't be worked out, there's breaking up. Romeo and Juliet, history's most famous teenage lovers, only lasted about three days. Most relationships that begin in early adolescence last longer than that, but few of them go on forever. Breaking up, as the song says, is very hard to do. If the relationship has been a sexual one, it's a great deal harder.

JUST FOR SEX?

'Good grief, Samantha,' said Kirsty scathingly, when her friend queried the fact that she'd had intercourse behind the school gym with a boy in their class whom neither particularly liked. 'It's only sex. I'm not going to marry him.'

Some young people don't seem to mind having casual sex.

It's essential for these boys or girls to accept that safe sexual practice – the use of condoms on every occasion and without exception – is absolutely essential. The pill does not protect a girl from sexually transmitted disease. They should also be aware that that sex is rarely, if ever, 'only sex', and that casual sex will sooner or later affect their emotional development.

'Nonsense,' said Kirsty to the doctor she relied on for her contraceptive pills. 'I know the difference between a relationship and a root. I just haven't got time to bother with a relationship right now and a root is entirely recreational.'

Some girls are so totally 'together', that they cope well enough with casual sex. With a strong personality and a great deal of confidence, they will name their own conditions before agreeing to oral sex (giving head, sucking a boy off) or intercourse.

But really, you'd have to wonder why.

And if they ever genuinely fall in love, you'd have to hope for their sake that their boyfriend didn't mind how many people had been there before him.

As for teenage boys – if they know a girl is offering no-risk, no-relationship sex, who would blame them for having a go? What would their mates think of them if they didn't?

Yes, but hey! What do they think of themselves?

Whether or not either of them realises it, casual sexual affairs hurt both of the people involved because their emotional needs are not met. Sooner or later, recreational rooting is likely to catch up with them.

One of the saddest things that is happening is that a lot of young people are having casual sexual encounters because of their emotional needs, because they need so badly to be loved, because they yearn so strongly to be close to another person.

Sex rarely if ever solves their problems. Instant sex is neither practical nor necessarily enjoyable. Sex with someone you've grown to love, in a situation that is neither rushed nor frantic nor riddled with guilt, in an atmosphere that is private and beautiful, is always so much better. Always. Especially afterwards.

BEWARE OF THE BOX!

The cheapest and most relaxed place for young people to get together is at home, and those whose parents welcome their friends may not realise how lucky they are. However, home has its limitations. For one thing, if a romance is happening, you don't want to be under the watchful eye of your parents – or worse still, your nosy sister who walks backwards up the hall so she can watch you kiss goodnight, or your ghastly brother who pops up behind the couch and rests his chin on his arms and just stares at you and grins.

Lots of kids hire videos and watch them in their family rooms in the absence of their cooperative mothers and fathers. In fact, 'pizza and a video' is probably the most common national recreation for young people in Australia.

So they watch more and more videos and live vicariously the lives of their screen heroes and heroines. Their expectations of love and romance grow and with these expectations come the delusions that often make their true-life romances so difficult to understand. It's fairly inevitable that some kids are tempted to try sex themselves. It's equally inevitable that they are frequently disappointed.

One of the problems of falling in love in our busy, media-flooded, stressed-out world is that young people expect instant perfect love. We live in a microwave, fast food, order-now-pay-later society. When kids want something, they want it *now*. And they want it to be just as good as it looked on the television.

Physical attraction might happen in an instant, but love – true, sincere, good love – tends to grow. Adolescents get very disappointed and disillusioned when they try to fall in love in the same way as the characters on the television screen. Their expectations don't come up to 'Melrose Place' standards.

You know, when advertising companies make commercials for crusty pies on television, they paint them with vaseline to make them glisten. It's not real but it makes you look and long for it. It's the same with sex on the screen. They make it look fabulous. It's not real but it makes you look and long for it.

Think about it. Don't believe everything you see.

'It's for you,' said Gregory, her white-faced, white-haired, white-livered little brother. 'It's a boy again. Why would any boy ring you? Does he need glasses?'

'Get a life,' she snarled at him as she took the phone. She waited until he sauntered off before she spoke. She hardly dared to breathe, she was hoping so much it would be Ben.

'Hi,' he said. 'I was wondering if you'd be allowed to go to the beach.'

Straight to the point, she thought. She loved the way he did that. So many people waffled on for ages before they got anywhere with their talking. It was such a waste of time.

'It's a bit cold,' she said, and then she could have kicked herself. What if he thought that meant she didn't want to go, didn't want to see him?

'I know,' he said. 'I didn't mean to swim. Just for a walk and maybe a look around the rocks. My mum's got to drive to the coast this afternoon. She can take us.'

She thought he must really like her, if he didn't mind his mum knowing about them.

They talked to each other every day now, at school. They talked at recess and at lunch. They talked about movies they'd seen and books they'd been made to read and what was happening at school; about how gloomy the television news was and how they had both discovered they enjoyed reading the newspapers; about their families and how different Ben's was to her split situation. Ben tried to imagine living in a house where there was hardly ever anyone home and you had to cook and clean and shop not only for yourself but for your dad and little brother as well; Lucy tried to imagine a life where the mother wore an apron over her jeans and cooked a meal every single night and the whole family sat around the dinner table and talked, sometimes until nine o'clock.

At first her friends had been around, talking about themselves as girls are inclined to do, and expecting everyone else, and Ben especially, to be interested in what they had to say. The guys in Ben's group sometimes drifted over. But people were finally getting the message. Ben and Lucy had a lot to say to each other and they had no time to listen to anybody else.

The girls, she knew, were thrilled, curious and a bit annoyed, all at once. They wanted details and she refused to give any. Ben said it was the same with him. His mates teased him and joked about him and Lucy going out together. But it was easier for him. Boys seemed to be able to insult and offend each other without anyone's feelings being hurt. Girls were always so obsessed with themselves at the expense of those around them; they loved talking about their emotions, and they would swear lifelong loyalty to each other one minute and then viciously stab a friend in the back as soon as she stepped over whatever was the accepted line for that week. Lucy had learned a lot about girls and their fragile friendships at her last two schools. She no longer threw herself into them. She had been hurt because she had trusted people too much, revealed too much about herself. Girls had taken what they knew about her feelings and used it against her. By the time they wanted to start a new episode in the tedious soap opera of their boring little lives by effecting a deeply meaningful reunion, she had grown tired of it all. Girls' relationships, she decided, were based on competition and jealousy and television plots. She wanted none of it. She'd seen enough of that at home.

Because of competition and jealousy and so-called love affairs, her mother now lived in another state and her father, despite a trail of women willing to help him recover from his divorce, was basically a very lonely man with a lot of bills to pay.

Lucy loved both her parents but she thought her father was a much nicer person than her mum, who had proved to them all that no matter how much she said she loved them, she couldn't be trusted. Her father was disorganised and easily led astray, Lucy thought, but unlike their mother, he had put his kids first. More than anything else, he wanted them with him – whereas their mother preferred her and Gregory in small doses that didn't interfere with her career or her social life. The fact is, Lucy thought, that with the exception of Gregory, she preferred males.

Especially Ben. Ben listened when she spoke and thought about what she said. Ben was never jealous when she did better than him in school. He wasn't angry or hurt when she teased and joked with his friends, which she did, occasionally, as she began to know them better. Ben wasn't easily led like her father – true to form, other girls flirted with him increasingly, once they knew there was something going on between him and Lucy. It was almost as if they thought he was like a tomcat on the prowl, she thought – he was interested in a female so surely any female would do. She loved the way he would look at them seriously while they spoke and then, when they were finished, he would turn back to her and rest his gorgeous big brown eyes on her face, and smile. It was as if he was flicking his own personal remote control through a variety of channels, watching a few seconds of each and then finding the program he wanted to settle down with for the rest of the evening.

He hardly ever smiled, but when he did it nearly knocked her out. He had fantastic white, even teeth (he said he owed them entirely to his orthodontist) and a bum chin, with the crease right in the middle, like Jon Bon Jovi's. He had pimples on his forehead and his cheeks but what did a bit of acne matter with a face as cute as his, with eyelashes so thick, and with a body so big and beautifully huggable.

She wanted to hug him all the time but so far all they had done was hold hands. He had wonderful hands, so big they covered hers entirely. Lucy had always watched a lot of television – there was never any adult around to tell her to stop or to supervise the classification of the programs she chose – and the love scenes were beginning to make her uncomfortable. Every time she saw two people kiss – and lots more besides – she couldn't help imagining it was her and Ben. Her pants would get quite damp and sometimes her breasts ached. One night, after watching a particularly graphic love scene, her vagina began to throb. She wondered if there was something wrong with her, or if she was showing signs of turning into a slut. Just in case it showed, she stopped masturbating in bed at night. Now that she had Ben, just thinking about him was enough.

THE SEX FILES: WHAT EVERYONE NEEDS TO KNOW

Because sex is the sort of subject that is titillating and embarrassing at the same time, many adolescents – and plenty of adults too, as a matter of fact – only have a sketchy idea of the sexual functions of their bodies. Even if you think you know everything about sex and sexuality, think of this chapter as a revision list. Perhaps you'll come across the occasional bit of information that fills a gap – the stuff you've forgotten or never knew, the things they didn't tell you up the back of the bus, the facts that drifted over your head during health period at school.

GETTING STARTED: PUBERTY

Puberty is a flash word for the physical developments involved in growing from a child into an adult. A lot of adults tend to associate it with bad tempers, sulking, tantrums, slammed doors and weird haircuts. Sometimes teenagers cash in on puberty as an excuse for acting crazy.

The journey to physical maturity is a long one, beginning as early as eight or nine in some children and finishing somewhere between those two big excuses for a booze up – the eighteenth and twenty-first birthdays. The trip to mental maturity can take a lot longer. Some people still haven't arrived at the age of forty-five. You see them on the roads every day, usually driving huge vehicles too fast. On the other hand, some adolescents develop serenity, self-confidence and rational judgment quite early on in their lives.

During puberty, boys and girls grow up in every sense of the word. They get taller and heavier and most of the organs in the body grow with them, the brain showing the least change. (No, Mums and Dads, don't say a *word*!) In fact, the brain has done most of its growing during early childhood.

Sexual development happens in five stages. Different young people experience these stages at different ages – there is no set rule about when body changes have to happen.

Stage one: In pre-pre-puberty nothing much shows, but the train to adulthood is at the station and in the engine room the changes are starting to chug into place.

Stage two: The first physical signs of growing up roll by. For girls, the breasts begin to bud and some little wisps of pubic hair appear around the vagina. For boys, this stage sees the growth of pubic hair and an increase in the size of their testicles and scrotum – the bag of skin in which the testicles grow.

Stage three: Girls' breasts continue to grow and the pubic hair thickens. Boys' testicles grow larger and their pubic hair thickens and meets across the top of the genital area. The penis increases in size.

The dreaded acne surfaces around this time. Affecting 85% of teenagers, blackheads and pimples (whiteheads) and in more severe cases, cysts, boils and pustules, are caused by hormones producing increased amounts of sebum, an oily substance found in the sebaceous glands in the skin. This results in the skin pores being easily blocked, trapping bacteria which leads to the skin breaking out.

A boy's semenarche occurs in stage three of puberty. Even very little boys can have an erection, although in childhood this is not generally connected with sexuality. The arrival of the semenarche means a boy's body starts producing semen, the whitish fluid in which sperm can travel. A boy is then capable of ejaculation. This means that when he is sexually aroused, his penis becomes stiff and erect and is capable of spurting sperm. It is the sperm that fertilises the female egg in order to make a baby.

Boys can now have 'wet dreams'. All this means is that they have sexy dreams which give them an erection and cause them to ejaculate while they are asleep. This is nothing to be embarrassed about. If anything, it's a reason to celebrate. Manhood is just around the corner.

Towards the end of stage three, girls and boys will both notice that the hair on their arms and legs is becoming thicker. Boys will start getting hair on their faces and chests. Girls might have a little more hair on their faces too. It's quite normal.

Stage four: Girls' pubic hair thickens and becomes coarse; it now grows in the shape of a triangle. Underarm hair also appears. The circle around the nipples, which is called the areola, becomes darker and slightly swollen, giving the breasts a more pointy appearance until stage five, when the tips of the breasts resume a more rounded shape.

The biggest change so far for a girl occurs during stage four, when she starts getting her periods – this is known as menstruation and the very first period is called the menarche. It refers to the flow of menstrual blood and tissue from the vagina, which occurs at regular intervals throughout a woman's reproductive life. In some cultures the menarche is a cause for celebration. Hooray! Womanhood has arrived! In our society, it is regarded as a messy and embarrassing development. It *is* messy, particularly at the beginning, when girls are not used to coping with the pads and tampons that are necessary to absorb the blood, but it is absolutely normal. It happens to virtually every woman in the world and is as natural as breathing.

Because periods are a remarkable event in a girl's sexual development, they will be explained in more detail later in this chapter.

A girl doesn't have to be finished with puberty in order to have a baby. If she has sexual intercourse with a male once she starts menstruating, she can become pregnant, although if she is only a young teenager and still growing, pregnancy is not good for her. Her body is still developing and being prepared by nature for the experience of bearing children.

For a boy in stage four of puberty, the penis has now grown quite a bit. He is likely to be getting facial hair and his voice may start breaking about now.

Stage five: The train has arrived. Girls and boys are now physically adults – their shape, size and body development are complete. Their brains, however, will continue to develop more gradually for another six or seven years.

BODY TALK

Girls and boys who know what's going on in their own bodies are much better equipped to deal with sex and sexuality. Here are the physical facts.

GIRLS

The female reproductive organs are inside the body, as opposed to the male's, which are on the outside and obvious to all. When it comes to their sexual development, this makes it harder for girls to understand what's going on.

THE FEMALE REPRODUCTIVE SYSTEM

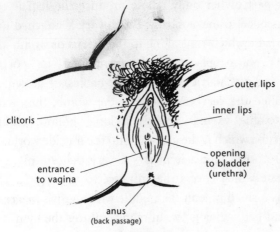

EXTERNAL VIEW

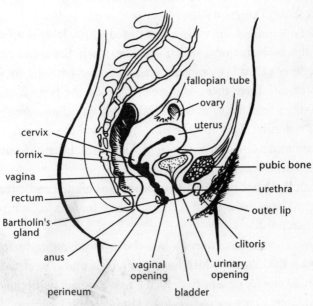

INTERNAL VIEW

A young, fully developed woman has two **ovaries** inside the lower part of her body. These produce the female egg which is needed to make a baby. Each ovary is attached to a **Fallopian tube** which runs along to the **uterus** or **womb**, the mysterious warm place, much mentioned in poetry, literature and psychiatric studies, where babies are grown. At a place called the **cervix**, or neck of the womb, the uterus opens into the **vagina**. This is a long, hollow, elastic, muscular tube which is the gateway into the outside world.

Girls are born with a **hymen** – a very delicate piece of elastic tissue which covers the entrance to the vagina. The hymen has a small hole in the middle which grows bigger as the girl and her vagina grow. In many cultures the hymen is regarded as proof of virginity. Because this issue is of particular interest to many young girls it is discussed in detail in *You Sexy Thangs* on page 98.

The opening of the vagina is enclosed by the **labia minora** and the **labia majora**, which are like small flaps, but are sometimes called lips or even petals. Together with the small layer of fat above them, the area in which the labia live is sometimes referred to as the vulva. The labia minora are the small red inner flaps and the labia majora are the outer ones and are more obvious, as they look like normal flaps of skin. Pubic hair first appears on the labia.

Both the labia contain lots of **sebaceous glands** and sweat glands. These make them a common site for lumps, bumps and infections.

Between the labia minora but above the opening of the vagina is the **clitoris,** which looks like a little bud. The clitoris is a small cluster of sensitive erectile tissue, 'sensitive' because it contains many nerve endings and 'erectile' because it becomes erect when a girl is aroused. It is covered by a tiny hood, which in a way is the equivalent of the foreskin which covers the male penis.

One poetic young person described the clitoris as 'the little man in the boat'.

Just below the clitoris is another opening, called the **urethra**, which is connected to the bladder. The urethra is not a sexual organ – it is for passing urine (wee). Between the vagina and the **anus** (the arse hole or bum hole) the skin tissue is very elastic. This is called the **perineum**. On either side of the perineum are the **Bartholin glands** which produce the lubricating fluid that makes intercourse easier.

Getting a big mirror and having a look at your genital area is a good way to become familiar with your own body. With clean hands and fingernails, feel the different textures of the skin that forms the labia, the clitoris and the glands. Test what feels good and what does not. If you'd rather not explore, that's cool too.

FEMALE CIRCUMCISION

In some parts of the world and among a variety of cultures, there is a practice known as female circumcision or female genital mutilation. This involves the cutting or removal of certain parts of girls' and women's external genitals. The procedures vary, but all are deeply rooted in traditional customs, together with a range of beliefs which have no medical basis but range from purity and cleanliness to contraception and, conversely, fertility. Women who have undergone the procedures in other countries now live in Australia. The practice is illegal in most states, although female genital mutilation may be carried out in very small numbers in some communities.

PERIODS

Menstruation is commonly referred to as 'having a period' because it's meant to happen to a girl at a definite time or period each month. During puberty, girls don't always get their periods regularly; it sometimes takes many months – even years – for the menstrual cycle to get into a rhythm.

Periods occur because once a girl begins developing into a woman, her body starts preparing to produce children. Once every month or so, the ovaries in her body produce an egg which has the potential, if fertilised by male sperm, to grow into a baby. This is called **ovulation.** The brain sends a message to the girl's uterus, or womb, reporting that an egg is on the way. The uterus then takes a few days to grow a lining, made of soft cells and tissue, to enable it to receive and nurture the egg when it arrives.

If no sexual intercourse takes place, no male sperm is received, so the egg is not fertilised. The brain sends a second message to this effect, so the uterus obligingly gets rid of the lining, which, with the egg, is shed from the body. The stuff that comes out through the vagina when a girl is having her period is not just blood – it is made up of blood, pieces of cell and bits of tissue. It usually comes out in a rush at first (what the television commercials call 'the heaviest days') and then peters out to a dribble. The whole process of menstruation takes from four to eight days.

The first day that bleeding begins is always taken as day one in a girl's menstrual cycle. Ovulation occurs twelve to fourteen days later. A few days after that, before her period is due, a girl may experience **PMS** or pre-menstrual syndrome. She may feel moody, cranky and emotional, even quite depressed. More than her usual share of pimples might pop out, or she might get some headaches. Her breasts may become sore and it's normal to feel bloated and slow at this time. Luckily, most of the symptoms wear off once the period begins, but it's not a good time to make critical decisions, like running away from home or leaving school or dropping your backpack from a three-storey building.

Period pain is another matter. No amount of medical science has yet been able to eliminate the intermittent stomach cramps that often go with menstruation, although girls taking the contraceptive pill often find this reduces the discomfort. Over-the-counter painkillers designed for period pain work moderately well for most people. Many girls never suffer from period pain but others get it quite badly. Some get a backache rather than a stomach-ache. Later on in life, when a girl has a baby, she will realise that period pain is very similar to birth pains, although much less intense. Like labour pains, period pain rarely last longer than twenty-four hours.

Periods used to be hugely inconvenient and difficult for girls to cope with, but modern technology has reduced a lot of the embarrassment and washing. **Pads** are now disposable, highly absorbent and easy to stick onto underpants. **Tampons** – internal pads shaped like cylinders which are pushed up into the vagina and pulled out with the fine string that is attached to them – are even more convenient and, once in there, cannot be felt at all.

It's perfectly all right for a young girl who has not had sex to use a tampon. Once a girl has a period, all the reproductive organs in her body are fully developed so the claim that girls in their early teens are 'too small' for tampons is not correct. The biggest problem is that inexperienced girls are probably not familiar with the shape and direction of their vaginas, which makes inserting the tampon difficult and potentially painful. It's important to be aware that the vagina slants upwards and backwards.

While putting tampons in can be quite difficult to do at first, it becomes wonderfully easy with practice and familiarity. It does! It really really does! Practising with them when you haven't got a period, using a lubricant like vaseline, will help. Feeling the way with your finger first is a good idea.

Pads and tampons need to be changed regularly, with the frequency depending on the heaviness of the blood flow. **Toxic shock** – an infection caused by bacteria forming on a tampon and releasing toxins or poisonous chemicals that are potentially deadly – is very rare, but tampons should be removed at least every six hours.

Tampons can't get lost, never to be seen again, as even if you have lost the string, they tend to expand and disintegrate once they become over-full. They are then likely to come out in rather smelly bits and pieces. Occasionally they do get stuck for a while, so to avoid the embarrassment of having to search for them, or getting medical assistance to locate them, you should always concentrate on making sure the string is protruding from the correct end when you put one in.

It's never a good idea to put used tampons down the toilet. Most public toilets provide receptacles for used pads and tampons. At home they should be wrapped in newspaper and put in the bin. A young plumber with a wavy undercut and an earring once pointed out, over a shovel full of grubby ex-tampons, that using them won't hurt your own plumbing but they can really wreck the household pipes.

If a sexually active young woman misses a period it may be

because she is pregnant. However, there can be other causes, including weight loss, a change in diet, anxiety, exercise, travel and illness.

Having intercourse without protection while menstruating is not a reliable way of avoiding pregnancy. Apart from that, while it is messier than usual, intercourse during a period does no harm to either the man or the woman.

BOYS

Boys' reproductive organs are external. The main feature is the **penis**, which contains the urethra, which carries **sperm** and urine. The penis is soft and limp when not erect. When a boy is aroused it becomes much larger and very firm. There's always been a lot of hot debate about the size of the erect penis, as well as its shape and angle, and how this affects a person's ability to perform intercourse. In fact, the size of the penis makes no difference at all to the male's ability to give pleasure or to produce sperm.

All boys are born with a **foreskin** or soft outer layer of skin which covers the penis. Some baby boys have their foreskin removed soon after birth. This is called **circumcision.** Whether a foreskin is present or not makes no difference to their sexual performance or to their sexual health. Obviously, if a boy has a foreskin, it has to be cleaned, just as longer hair or longer-than-usual nails need to be kept clean.

Behind the penis are two **testicles** which live in the **scrotum,** a loose sack-like layer of skin. The testicles produce the sperm which is necessary for reproduction. Both testicles are connected to the rest of the body through a number of structures, but mainly by two tubes, one on each side, called

THE MALE REPRODUCTIVE SYSTEM

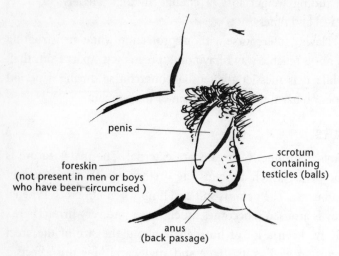

penis

foreskin
(not present in men or boys
who have been circumcised)

scrotum
containing
testicles (balls)

anus
(back passage)

EXTERNAL VIEW

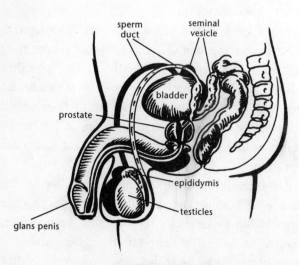

sperm
duct

seminal
vesicle

bladder

prostate

epididymis

glans penis

testicles

INTERNAL VIEW

the **vas deferens**. These carry the sperm into the **urethra**. The urethra is a long tube which delivers both urine and sperm through the penis and out into the world (although not at the same time). On the way to the penis, the vas deferens pass the **prostate gland**, from where they collect some **seminal fluid,** or **semen**, a thick whitish substance which carries the sperm along. When a boy ejaculates, this is the fluid that spurts out.

The urethra also connects to the bladder, and carries **urine** out of the body. However, boys cannot wee and ejaculate sperm at the same time.

GETTING TURNED ON

LUST

It is very possible for boys and girls – and men and women as well – to be turned on without being in love.

A lot can happen along the way to puberty. By the time a boy reaches the third stage of puberty he is capable of sexual feelings and he can be sexually aroused, which means his heart beats faster and his penis becomes erect. What happens when a boy is aroused is that his brain sends messages that speed up his blood flow, in particular the flow of blood to his penis. The penis, engorged with blood (not with semen, as some people think), becomes big and hard. When this happens, the veins which would normally return that blood back into the arteries are automatically blocked off, so that the penis remains erect, getting bigger and harder as more blood is pumped into it.

A girl is more likely to feel sexually aroused when she reaches the fourth stage of puberty – after she starts getting her period. When a girl feels turned on, the blood flow in her body speeds up, her heart beats faster, her pupils may dilate and she often gets goosebumps. Her nipples may become erect (although other feelings, like being cold, can cause this too). The increased flow of blood to her genital area causes her clitoris and vagina to become swollen. Extra fluid seeps from the surrounding cells into her vagina, which becomes damp. This may produce a throbbing or thumping feeling between her legs. The extra moisture is provided by nature to prepare a female for sexual intercourse. If she has sex, it is this fluid or lubricant which carries the male fluid, containing the sperm, up into her uterus, where an egg lies waiting to be fertilised.

For a girl, this rush of blood, this throbbing feeling, can feel very nice. However, it can also be very intense and, because of the pressure, even quite painful.

The old-fashioned word for these feelings and reactions in both girls and boys is 'lust'. The closest modern expression for it is probably being 'turned on'. All sorts of stimulating things can cause lust, from the sight of a gorgeous, sexy person to music, food, alcohol, drugs, perfume, pictures – even dreams. Cuddling, touching bodies, kissing and stroking can create or intensify lust. Even just being close to someone lovely can do it, which is often very embarrassing for boys, who have little control over the sudden appearance of a bulge in their trousers.

Frustratingly, the time of the month when a girl's desire for sex may be very strong is the most dangerous time of all for her to have intercourse, as the possibility of pregnancy is greatly increased. This is when her body fluids are ready to flow fast; inside her system there's an egg hurtling towards her uterus in the expectation that it will be fertilised by the first male sperm that swims that way.

For hundreds of years, people have been getting lust confused with love. Lust is definitely not love. Day dreams, movies, stories and all sorts of sexual stimulants, from being stroked and fondled to riding a horse or even travelling along a bumpy road in a car while thinking about your boyfriend, can cause lust – whereas love depends on friendship, affection, mutual respect, admiration, thoughtfulness, sharing and caring about each other.

The main problem with lust is that it doesn't last very long, but it gets a lot of people into a lot of trouble along the way. Many pregnancies are the result of lust, not love. Millions of hearts have been broken because one lover is in love but the other one is simply in lust. It's not always easy to tell the difference.

MASTURBATION

Sexual feelings during puberty can be very intense, although young people are not likely to do anything about them with anyone else for some time. What they can do is masturbate – to explore and sexually stimulate their own bodies.

Masturbation is the stimulation of your genitals using your own hands, fingers or even some other object until you reach orgasm. Not many years ago, 'playing with yourself' was considered to be not only unhealthy but downright disgusting. In a more enlightened era, we know that touching, feeling and exploring your own genital area is normal and is also a very safe way of learning about your own body. It can be a very pleasurable pastime, but it is also a very private experience. Nobody knows how many people, let alone young people, masturbate.

Masturbation is totally safe – there is no such thing as over-masturbating and you cannot catch a disease or become pregnant. And as David Bennett reminds us in his book *Growing Pains,* you don't have to look your best to do it. Pleasuring yourself in this way can reduce sexual tension and teach you more about yourself. However, like any sexual act, it's not compulsory. If it doesn't feel good, don't do it.

FANTASY

The only sexual act that's even safer than masturbation is fantasy. Whether you are thinking about something sexy, or reading about it, or talking about it to someone you trust, or dreaming about it while you play your favourite music, it's all yours. Your dreams and imaginings and wonderings are your own, to play with as you please. There's no need for guilt or worry. There is a huge difference between what you do and what you think about. So choose anyone you like and experiment with your feelings by making love to them in your mind. Let your imagination go wild. Enjoy yourself.

The sea was slate grey but never still; millions of white-capped waves kept it dancing. Lucy and Ben walked along the shore with their jackets zipped tightly against the winter wind. Ben's mother was doing some charity business with a woman who lived in a beach house on the cliff; she said to meet her there at four. They had two hours to walk and talk and just be together.

At the far end of the beach they stopped and sat down, huddling together in the shelter of the rocks. After all their imaginings and dreams, it was so easy. They didn't even hurry. They looked at the sea for what seemed a very long time, and he stroked her hand, first the outside, then the palm, with his long, strong fingers. She asked him if he'd ever learned the piano and he said he had and told her how he'd still be playing if only his teacher had let him try more jazz. But while he spoke he was resting his eyes on her face in that special way that turned her stomach to churned butter, and neither of them was listening to what he had to say. He knew he was going to kiss her and she knew she was going to kiss him and after a while, that's what happened.

Her lips were so soft. He couldn't believe such softness.

His lips were so soft. She hadn't thought a boy's lips would be as soft as that.

They drew apart and looked at each other. Then she smiled. He smiled back. They were in love with each other's smiles. The wind whipped their hair around their faces. Their big jackets rustled as they slid their arms around each other and enjoyed a huge hug. It felt so good. So right.

After a while a man walked past with his scrawny dog and they dropped their arms and walked back along the beach the way they had come. The held hands and talked about what they had thought about when they first noticed each other.

'I thought you were never going to smile at me,' said Lucy. Ben grinned at his sneakers, plodding along in the wet sand. They both started laughing. He stopped walking and kissed her again, but she was still laughing so he actually kissed her teeth and some of her hair which was blowing into her mouth. They both spluttered and laughed more. It was wonderful that it didn't matter.

Later, in the car, he sat in the back seat with her and held her hand. His mum said she felt like a chauffeur and turned the radio up loudly and sang Beatles songs, slightly off-key, all the way home.

AMIRA'S STORY

What were you expecting? When you were looking for a virgin, a girl over twenty-one who knew her own mind and heart, how did you picture her? When all the giggles and sighs and snide asides subsided, when you heard her breathless, husky voice on the telephone, what image sprang to mind?

Certainly not this tall, lissom creature, this lush, full figure, hugged by a clinging V-necked T-shirt, these long legs in tailored navy jeans. Certainly not the face of an eastern princess, heart-shaped, cream-skinned, even featured, dominated by enormous dark eyes, framed by glossy blue-black hair. Certainly not this aura of serenity, this happy contentment, this acceptance of the way she is and the way she expects life to be.

Amira is twenty-one years old, a Maronite Catholic, a university student – and a virgin. According to her, she is a long way from being unique.

'I was born in Australia but when I was seven my parents sold up almost everything they had and moved back to Lebanon. It didn't work out for them. It was war time and everything. So ten months later we came back here. They moved into a flat and started from scratch. My Dad is a very hard worker so in the thirteen years since we've been back he's been building up his business so we could have a good life again.

My Dad built this house. We had the land already – it was the one thing they didn't sell when they left, which shows you how smart my parents are. We've lived here for about twelve years.

I went to a Catholic school and now I'm at university, doing a Bachelor of Education, majoring in computers. I'd like to be a teacher. I know I can help kids. I have lots of cousins. I can talk to them all. I can talk to anybody and everybody and they always listen to me and talk back with me. I make an effort to talk to people and I don't think a lot of others do that these days. They keep to themselves.

I like talking to boys as well as girls. My school was a co-educational school, there were plenty of boys there and I meet boys at university and of course there are lots of guys at the parties and gatherings we have with the local Lebanese community. Also I have two brothers as well as a sister. I'm not scared of boys at all. The only thing is that if I really like a guy I won't approach him. I guess I'm scared of rejection. Maybe.

We had some sex education at school. In Year Five, when I was ten, the school principal, who was a nun, came in and told us about how our bodies would change, and about getting periods and all that. The boys were put into another classroom to hear from a male teacher what would happen to them.

I think we all took it pretty seriously, even though we were so young. I did anyway. I had never thought about it before. I'd never heard it discussed at home or anywhere, but being the eldest, that's probably why.

Then in Year Seven, in high school, they told us in health class about the differences between males and females. They didn't actually talk about having sex, about the act itself. I remember the teacher saying to us: "We're not allowed to tell you about sex because this is a Catholic School. But if you ask me a question I am obliged to answer you correctly." One kid put up her hand and asked about condoms and she did give a proper answer, but that was that. Nobody else asked any questions. During the year, when other girls started menstruating and I didn't, I started to wonder why it wasn't happening to me. Mum spoke to me about it after a while, when she could see I was really worried. She said, you know, one day you'll have a period. And that was that, really. That was the only time sexuality has ever been mentioned. I have never had a sit-down formal discussion about sex with either of my parents. Never.

But it didn't worry me. I mean, when my body started to change, when my breasts started getting larger and the other things happened, I just knew it was normal. I just felt it was finally happening to me, just like they had said it would, and now I was like all my friends. I looked at myself and I touched myself, which I think is all perfectly normal.

There was no more sex education after that. I never heard it mentioned in the senior years of high school. Not by the teachers, I mean.

People say kids learn about sex from their friends but with my friends, that's not the sort of thing we ever talk about. I have very close friends who I see every day and we talk about everything that happens to us. If one of us met a nice guy we would be on the phone straight away. But we don't talk about sex.

The thing, is we all know where we stand. We've all agreed we're not going to have sex before we get married, so it's not an issue for us. I can't think of a single close friend of mine who has ever even considered having sex with anyone, even the ones who have steady boyfriends. One of my best friends is engaged but that hasn't changed the way she feels about intercourse.

You do see a lot of sex stuff on television, you see it all the time. But that's just TV, it's not real life. What would they make the shows about if only the married couples slept together?

I have a part-time job in an office and I'm the youngest person there. There's a guy of twenty-two and a secretary who is twenty-eight, who is a really nice person, and the boss is only twenty-five. They talk about their sex lives all the time and I can't help feeling a bit embarrassed. They've started saying: "Time to shut your ears, Amira," before they start.

I can't remember ever making a decision to remain a virgin until I married. It's just taken for granted, it's the way I've been brought up. I haven't considered anything else. It's what I want. I want sex to be really special, with the right person. I would never consider having casual sex, just for the sake of it.

I suppose you could call me a religious person. I go to church every Sunday and I follow my family's beliefs. I pray every night and I believe in God. Well, I believe Someone is there, watching over us. But I don't know how much influence that has on my decision to remain a virgin. I actually think it has a lot more to do with my friends. If you hang out with a group of people who behave in a particular way, you are more likely to want to do whatever they are doing. Because I have a close group of friends who strongly believe that sex should only happen within marriage, that has moulded my thinking. And family has a big influence, too.

The family talk about relationships – they discuss who has a girlfriend or a boyfriend, they encourage us to mix with people of the opposite sex. But they don't mention sex at all – that just doesn't come up.

In my culture, if a girl is known to have slept around, people will think a lot less of her than they will of a guy who has done the same thing. It's nothing if a guy does it.

I've thought about it. If I really loved a man, and we were planning to marry, I might consider sleeping with him. But then again, I still think it would be best to wait so it would be really special on the wedding night.

The situation hasn't arisen anyway, because I haven't had a serious boyfriend. I've been very close friends with one guy, but there was nothing sexual in our relationship.

Boys come and pick me up and take me places but we mainly go out and meet others. We mix in big groups. In the Lebanese community, everyone is related or connected in one way or another. Because of that, I've met heaps of guys. They try to talk to me. They call me on the phone. After a few calls I tend to back off a bit. Most of my friends are getting steady boyfriends now. One of my closest friends used to ring me every day and now that she has a boyfriend I never hear from her. I see my friends going off with their guys and I sometimes think it would be nice to have someone like that – just to go out, just to have someone to talk to.

People say I'm too fussy and I don't give guys a chance. But I don't think that's the case. Some people think I'm scared but I'm not. I am quite confident in what I believe. Certainly if I went out with a guy and he pressured me to have sex with him, I would know he wasn't the right person for me.

My situation worries other people more than it worries me. My friends and relatives are inclined to say: "Oh Amira, you're twenty-one and you haven't got a boyfriend." I just think: "So?" Of course I have times when I feel low. But so does everybody.

I believe everyone has the right to choose how they want to live. If somebody sleeps with their girlfriend or boyfriend, that's their right and their choice. They are not hurting me.

Sometimes when I watch sex scenes on television I wonder what it would be like. Sometimes my cousins ask me if I'm frustrated. I'm not, I don't think I am. Sometimes I masturbate.

We have a good time at home. We talk about all sorts of things. We have our fights, but the good times far outweigh the bad. Mum and Dad are very affectionate with each other – Mum is shy but Dad isn't and he cuddles her and teases her. There are lots of special occasions to celebrate and we all go out together as well and we have a wonderful time. I love my family.

I've just about finished uni now, thank goodness. I'm glad I stuck it out, even though about half-way through I was ready to quit. I'm so grateful to my dad for persuading me to stay.

I'm really looking forward to being a teacher. I won't just be teaching kids about maths and computers, I will be a role model for them as well. Teachers are like a second set of parents and kids are influenced by them whether they realise it or not.

Students will listen to what I say. They may even look up to me. I've been thinking about it a lot. My students may never remember what I teach them about computers but they'll remember what they learn from me about life. It's an enormous responsibility.

I've thought about sex a lot too – another huge responsibility. I've wondered what it will be like. Scary, I think, but it will be something to share with the person I love. I think it will be very enjoyable for me but I truly believe it's well worth the wait. If it's with the right person, it's going to be the *best* thing.'

Lucy, whose young life had fallen far short of perfect, could not believe how perfect falling in love could be. They were back at the beach, in their favourite place among the rocks. Ben's mum was up in the cliff house, having another one of her meetings – this was the fourth Saturday that she'd invited them to come with her. Ben was lucky to have a mum who was so understanding, Lucy thought. It wasn't as easy as some people seemed to think, finding a place where two kids could be together without heaps of other people interrupting them.

Today the sun was shining and as soon as they had reached their rocks they had started kissing. Everything was exactly as she had dreamed – even the waves were crashing on the beach in time with the symphony in her head. Deep down low in her body it was as if other, invisible waves were rolling, rippling from her lips to her heart to her stomach, growing stronger as they rocked her body. He tightened his arms around her and she grasped his heavy jacket and pulled him as close as she could. Kissing Ben was like tasting heaven. He smelled nice. His lips tasted delicious. There was nothing messy or ghastly about it as there had been with other boys who had pressed their mouths against hers at parties, causing her to bite her own lips or making it essential to keep them tightly closed to hold their choking tongues at bay. Amateurs. Stupid kids. Nothing like Ben, who obviously knew what he was doing. Nothing like gentle Ben, who took his time, and not only about smiling.

But it wasn't enough. Why was he waiting so long? She opened her lips. Come in, come in, she thought, knowing she shouldn't, hoping he wouldn't, hoping he would.

His arms were a warm circle and his soft lips moved around hers. She thought she might burst if she couldn't have more of him. She saw women, writhing in desire in a million images on her television screen. Now she knew. Now she understood. She pressed herself into Ben's big body and ran the tip of her tongue along the inside of his top lip.

Then Lucy's perfect world fell apart. In a swift, panic-stricken movement, Ben pushed her away and jumped to his feet. He turned his back on her and walked away, making a great fuss of brushing sand off himself. When he turned back he was frowning. He offered her a hand to pull her up. She took it, he yanked her into standing position and then he dropped her hand as if it was a snake.

'Come on,' he said. 'Mum will be waiting.' He strode off and she had to run to keep up with him. Her mind was muddled with questions and panic. What had she done? What was it? What was wrong? Why had he stopped kissing her? Why? Why? Why?

YOU SEXY THANGS: WHAT, WHERE AND WHY STUFF HAPPENS

It's only quite recently that people have begun learning not to take the loveliness of nature for granted. They've become aware of the dangerous and destructive results that come from helping themselves to what they want whenever they want it, without protecting the environment, without respecting it or giving anything back in return.

Sexuality needs to be respected and protected as well. Once girls and boys become sexual beings, they also have to be responsible for the consequences of their sexual activities.

Sexuality is a fluid, changeable force which can bring peace and calm one day, stormy passion the next and love and laughter a week or so later. Sexual feelings vary enormously from one person to another. Sex is not the most important thing in life – indeed, for older people who are raising a family, managing a home and earning a living, it often plays a regrettably small role. But sex is always a very precious part of life, particularly for young people who are just beginning to sample the pleasures and passions sexuality has in store for them.

AGE OF CONSENT

In all states and territories of Australia, there are laws that determine the 'age of consent' to sex. This is the age at which it becomes legal for young people to engage in penetrative sexual acts. In New South Wales the age of consent is sixteen for heterosexuals of both sexes, but eighteen for homosexual young men. It's much the same in Western Australia. In the Australian Capital Territory and Victoria, the age of consent is sixteen for both heterosexual and homosexual sex. However, in Victoria, children aged between ten and sixteen can have sex if both people consent and providing the two young people are either married or not more than two years apart in age.

In South Australia and Tasmania, the age of consent for heterosexual and homosexual sex is seventeen, although SA law stipulates that both the young people involved must be seventeen or older. In Queensland and the Northern Territory, the age of consent is sixteen for girls; there is no age of consent for heterosexual boys. For homosexual boys it is eighteen.

THE VIRGINITY QUESTION

The loss of virginity has been regarded for centuries as the loss of innocence. Perhaps for this reason, the sexual state of young women – and, to a lesser degree, young men – continues to be a topic of fascination. It's commonly believed that purity is no longer valued as much as it used to be. For example, during the research for this book, the subject that most amused everyone involved was the quest for a virgin girl who had passed her eighteenth birthday.

In fact, there are plenty of virginal young women in Australia, and they are intelligent and beautiful as well!

There are also many boys who have put some intelligent thoughts into their personal development and have decided to wait until they are older, wiser and more self-sufficient before having sex. Unfortunately, no matter how sensible their decision is – not to mention how much trouble and grief it will save them in the long term – most boys can't help feeling embarrassed about their virginity. They may boast or lie about their sexual experience, which leads even more guys to believe they must be the last ones their age in town not to have 'done it'. Some boys feel so bad about not having sex that they get seriously depressed and somehow convince themselves that they are abnormal.

One of the most disappointing aspects of our supposedly enlightened society is that boys are made to feel that ridding themselves of their virginity is an essential part of becoming a man. It's not. Good sex with someone you love is well worth waiting for.

There are really two kinds of virginity. The traditional view is that a virgin is a girl or boy who has never had sexual intercourse. In other words, when a girl's vagina is penetrated by a male penis for the first time, she is no longer a virgin. When a boy's penis penetrates a vagina (or, in homosexual sex, an anus) for the first time, he is no longer a virgin.

For girls, the question of virginity still revolves very much around their hymen, the thin membrane that covers the opening of the vagina.

The hymen serves no obvious purpose, but in the past it has caused a huge amount of problems and it continues to do so in certain cultures today. In fact, it must be assumed from letters to *Dolly* and *Girlfriend* magazines that even modern young Australian women are still worrying and wondering about it.

Some people believe that when a girl is penetrated for the first time, the hymen will be torn and she will bleed. In fact, the hymen doesn't get broken – it already has a small hole in its centre and, once pierced, this hole simply stretches and grows, making the entry point to the vagina bigger.

The hymen is easily pierced during childhood or adolescence – having a nasty fall, riding a bike or horse, sitting astride a fence, during a medical examination – any of these events and many others could do it, but it may also remain intact until the first time a woman experiences intercourse. Some young women may bleed a little when they first have sex but many do not. Even if they have an intact hymen, it doesn't have many blood vessels in it so it might not bleed at all.

Any pain experienced by a young woman during intercourse is likely to be caused by nervous fear of the unknown – she can't help tensing up, which means the muscles around her vagina stiffen, making penetration more difficult. Also, just as fear gives some people a dry throat, anxiety causes dryness in the vagina as well, delaying the production of the lubricating moisture that makes intercourse so much smoother and more enjoyable.

Some adults might say a girl or boy cannot be 'a little bit virgin', any more than a girl can be 'a little bit pregnant'. However, a gentler view is that virginity depends on the way a young person has been involved in sexual activity. If a girl or boy has been sexually abused or assaulted or forced to have sex, and if they have never had a sexual experience in a mutually caring relationship, they could still be considered virgins.

At the other extreme, if a girl has had lesbian experiences with women, or a boy or girl has tried a variety of sexual acts without actually engaging in penis–vagina penetration, they may technically be virgins but they are certainly not innocent!

SAFE AND HAPPY

Sex doesn't just mean intercourse. Many young people who claim they haven't had sex or say they have decided not to have sex any more are referring only to intercourse – or to rooting, screwing or fucking, whatever term they use.

In reality, sexuality can be expressed in a whole variety of ways. A girl looking at a boy in the classroom at school, and tilting her head as she catches his eye, is expressing her sexuality. An elderly grandad taking his wife's hand is doing the same thing.

For most kids, sexuality starts with long looks, downcast eyes, flicked hair, hands accidentally brushing against each other, the not-so-casual resting of her hand on his arm for just a minute, the not-so-spontaneous removal by him of a leaf that's caught in her hair. Sometimes it even starts with a playful push or punch.

Holding hands can be the *best* thing when it comes to expressing sexuality. When two hands finally meet, fingers playing and pausing and then linking so neatly together, it may be the happiest and most satisfying feeling you can ever remember having.

Yet kissing can be even better. It's incredible that lips can be so soft, so yielding. Feelings can be conveyed silently, yet perfectly, in a kiss.

Kissing should always begin with lips alone. That's romance. Anyone who knows what they are doing will keep the tongue in check until they can be sure that deeper and more intimate kissing will be welcome. It's wise to remember that gentle probing with a tentative tongue can be exciting, but an unwelcome thrusting tongue can be a total turn-off.

Hugging is great. Hugging makes you feel warm and wanted. Cuddling up on a couch, snuggling with someone special, holding hands, stroking hair, stroking cheeks, tracing a path through the glossy hairs on his arm – that's sexuality. That's feelings. And none of that is going to get kids into trouble.

MOVING RIGHT ALONG...

The only thing that makes kissing and cuddling risky is that given the right situation – mainly an absence of adults – it often leads to more intimate activity. Kissing becomes prolonged, mouths open and the tongues get busy with each other. This often leads to what the sexperts call 'light petting' – touching or stroking the breasts and genitals, usually through the clothes.

Heavy petting is best left to mature couples in committed relationships, mainly because it usually leads to intercourse. It involves touching, exploring, licking and sucking of breasts and genitals either under or without clothes. This is more commonly known as foreplay, as it usually stimulates and excites the lovers to a point where the desire for intercourse is intense, urgent and difficult to resist.

GOING ALL THE WAY

Normal sexual intercourse happens when the penis enters the vagina. This joins the two bodies in a uniquely intimate way. The man then moves his penis backwards and forwards in a stroking motion which usually becomes faster and faster and can last for a minute or two or for longer, depending how long it takes him to reach his climax. The movement is made easier by the fluid secreted within the vagina.

The ultimate stimulation of both penis and vagina causes the man to reach a point where he ejaculates sperm or 'comes' into the woman.

If he is wearing a condom, the sperm remains within the protective covering.

For a couple who love each other, care about each other and are planning to remain together, this ultimate act of sexuality can be one of total abandonment and joy. To kids experimenting with sex, intercourse can cause a lot of problems.

The main physical risks are pregnancy and sexually transmitted diseases. Of all the STDs, the HIV virus, which can lead to AIDS, is probably the most life-threatening and the best publicised, but there are plenty of others that are common, painful and easily caught. Intercourse should never be attempted without the use of condoms. Even if the young woman is taking a contraceptive pill or using another contraceptive device, the risk of infection by sexually transmitted diseases is serious.

The other big risk for teenagers indulging in intercourse is not physical but emotional. The sexual act is not the same as eating and drinking and going to the toilet. It is a very intimate, very private union of two totally separate individuals. There is no other act which joins a man and a woman in this way. Because of this, intercourse involves feelings and emotions that last for a long time after the act itself. Young people who indulge themselves in casual sexual intercourse with people they don't know well – or even with people they know but certainly don't love – can damage the way they relate to others.

ORGASM

Orgasm, the physical climax of the sexual act, is a popular topic in glossy magazines and is often pantingly depicted on large and small screens as being the highlight of love-making. Also referred to as 'reaching the climax' or simply 'coming', orgasm in young men can be easily confused with ejaculation.

In males, ejaculation of sperm and orgasm do tend to occur at about the same time; usually, one very quickly follows the other. However, a young man can ejaculate without having an orgasm, and he can have an orgasm without ejaculating.

Orgasm for both sexes is a very intense, pleasurable sensation, created by the rapid contraction of the muscles around the genitals. For men, the contractions at the base of the penis are usually followed by the ejaculation of semen. In women, orgasm is caused by the involuntary rapid contraction of the muscles of the uterus and vagina. It's a sort of open-shut, open-shut sensation which quivers through the whole body, eventually slowing down and easing off. (*Involuntary* means nature causes the contractions – the woman just has to enjoy it. When women create an artificial orgasm by squeezing their genital muscles – or by vocally reacting to how fabulous they feel, as in the famous café scene in the movie *When Harry Met Sally* – this is known as faking it.)

Sexual enjoyment and fulfilment do not depend on reaching orgasm. Unfortunately, orgasm has become such a popular topic in the sex-driven media that some men and women believe that unless orgasm is achieved by both people, the whole sex thing has been a waste of time. This is not so, and for young people who are just making their way into the confusing business of bodies and feelings, whether or not the young woman reaches a climax is the least of their worries. As Terry Colling says in his book *Teenagers*, sex is more than just thrashing around until you get an orgasm. 'If the only object of sexual intercourse is to have an orgasm, then masturbation is much safer and easier.'

Orgasm is not purely physical. It's a psychological act. It's all mixed up with feelings and with what is going on between the man and the woman who are making love to one another. Orgasm is also affected by the amount of foreplay that has preceded intercourse. Foreplay stimulates and excites lovers. Males are easily stimulated but it takes longer for this to happen to females. Women need to tell their partners what they like them to do. The old-fashioned belief that men know more about turning a woman on and about sex generally is nonsense. Couples have to learn about sexuality, preferably from each other.

Orgasm is very much connected with the absolute abandonment of yourself to the physical thrill, the love, the pleasure – yes, and the lust – which the sexual act can produce. But abandonment to pleasure and fulfilment is usually only possible when you truly know and trust the person to whom you are making love and who is making love to you. When you are a teenager, this sort of trust and experience is pretty rare.

KIDS WHO WAIT

A serious long-term relationship is the best basis for 'going all the way' and, even then, young people in committed relationships are wise to content themselves with less dangerous ways of expressing their affection. They have decided that full-on sex should wait until they are old enough to thoroughly enjoy themselves without having to concern themselves with all the complications that go with it. Many young people, and especially those who live according to their religious beliefs, choose to wait for the permanence of marriage. Waiting doesn't spoil sexuality – in fact in a million ways it makes the real thing much better when it happens.

There are many very normal girls and boys who think this way. According to statistics, more than half of seventeen and eighteen year olds who are still at school, and 80% of Year Ten students, have not had sexual relationships.

Of course they still flirt. They kiss. They cuddle. They might wonder if they are in love. They sometimes get hurt. Who doesn't? From time to time they feel frustrated. Who doesn't? They recover. They play sport. They go to the movies. They hang out with friends, usually people with similar standards to their own. Most of all, they fantasise. They dream. With sex, a great deal of the pleasure is in the anticipation.

They hope that when they fall in love with the person they want to stay with forever, the sex will be special.

They wait.

OTHER OPTIONS

Anal intercourse is the term given to the penis entering the anus. This can happen between a male and a female or in homosexual sex, between two males. The anus is made up of tight little rings of muscle, called sphincters. Unlike the muscles in the vagina, these are not elastic, so it can be painful when the penis goes in, although once inside, the area within the bottom is elastic. The more it's done, the less it hurts.

Oral sex means stimulating the other person's genitals using the mouth and tongue. **Fellatio,** or giving head, is the term that describes the woman (or in homosexual male relationships, one of the men) taking the penis into her mouth and licking and/or sucking it, usually until the man reaches the point of ejaculation. Swallowing semen won't do any harm, although if the man wears a condom, this can be avoided. Fellatio will not cause pregnancy or illness. The possibility of catching the HIV virus through fellatio would be present only if there were cuts or abrasions on a woman's lips or mouth so that infected semen could enter her bloodstream. Some young women who refuse to have sexual intercourse with boys feel pressured to offer fellatio as a sort of consolation prize. No girl or boy should be pressured or forced to perform any sexual act on anyone else. If they don't want to do it, it is their right to say no.

Cunnilingus is the word for the male (or in lesbian relationships, one of the females) using his mouth and tongue to stimulate the girl's clitoris.

A **sixty-niner** is a modern term describing two people giving oral sex to each other simultaneously. They lie head to tail (resembling the number 69), so that each person's mouth is in contact with the other person's genitals.

It is possible to put fingers, hands or even a fists into the vagina to provide sexual stimulation. Some people put man-made or natural objects in there and a variety of **sex toys** are designed for insertion into the female body.

Common sense hygiene rules apply when experimenting in this way. Anything going into your body should be clean. This means washing hands and keeping fingernails short, as well as washing foreign matter. Nothing should be left inside for too long.

Never do anything that hurts. If soreness or pain result from your sexual experiments, stop.

SEX AND DRUGS

The biggest myth of all the stories associated with sexuality is the belief that sex and drugs go well together.

Alcohol is responsible for more of life's tragedies than anyone dares to imagine. Drugs like marijuana ('all you need is love') and ecstasy ('the love drug') which poison the brain with delusions about love and sexual prowess are capable of causing anything from simple silliness to death. Yes, death. At the age of fifteen, Anna Wood, one of many Australian teenagers who died from the effects of illegal drugs in 1995, wrote in her diary: 'How come I never find anyone? All my friends have guys but me... One day hopefully, the guy of my dreams will slide into my life.' Ecstasy killed this beautiful young woman before she ever had the chance to fall in love.

Young people who have sex under the influence of drink or drugs can't remember if they enjoyed themselves or not, or if they took precautions or not, or if they liked the person they did it with or not. They wake up (if they are lucky) with headaches or nausea or with whatever side effects their drug of choice has left them – and no idea of what the sex was for or why they did it. Many don't remember if they did it at all.

Whole towns could be populated with the babies born to girls and boys who had sex under the influence of alcohol. Sexually transmitted diseases love drug-takers and thrive in their bodies because these are the kids who are too high to protect themselves and too low to protect the people they are pretending to 'love'. For those who seem to escape scot-free from drug-induced sexual encounters there is still the vacuum best described by Helen in her story later in this book: 'I was so high I don't remember anything about it, whether it was painful, what we did, nothing. When I woke up the next morning I didn't have a clue where I was. You wake up and you think: "What have I done?" And he walks in and gives you a big smile and you think: "Oh no! Biggest mistake of my life." '

Medical evidence now shows that alcohol and illegal drugs harm the human reproductive system and may affect growth. In boys the level of testosterone is decreased for up to twenty-four hours after using alcohol or common illegal drugs such as marijuana. Continued heavy drug and alcohol use results in problems with impotence (the inability to get an erection) in 80% of boys. Research in the United States and Australia also indicates that illicit drug use may cause the depression of masculine sexual secondary characteristics – in other words, the growth of those features that turn a boy into a man is slowed down. There is less growth in the shoulders, there is more breast development than is normal in males and the pubic hair above the genitals starts growing in a triangular shape, so that it looks more like a girl's. Boys who smoke dope also have a depressed sperm count – their little guys swim a lot more slowly, because they are stoned. In some cases, babies fathered by these boys are born with defects. Boys who stop using illicit drugs return to normal with appropriate medical treatment.

Girls who use alcohol or illegal drugs before or during puberty may wait in vain to begin menstruating. Because of the negative effect drug use has on the ovaries (where the female eggs are created), girls who have begun menstruating may experience irregularity or their periods may stop altogether. Young women who drink heavily or regularly use illegal drugs risk developing masculine secondary characteristics – broad shoulders, narrow hips and more hair on the face. If a girl who drinks heavily or uses drugs regularly conceives a child, there is a serious possibility of the baby being born with foetal alcohol syndrome or, in the case of drugs, with a very low birth weight. The baby can also be born already addicted to its mother's drug of choice.

One of the worst effects of drugs is that they obscure the memory. This means if a girl or boy makes a mistake and has sex under the influence of alcohol or drugs, they will quite possibly make the mistake again – and again. The drugs give them total blockout – and they never learn or profit from their mistakes.

In our culture it's normal for girls and boys in early adolescence to hang out with kids of the same sex. Girls may talk a lot about boys and fantasise about love and romance, but the people they are closest to are the girlfriends who are on the same wavelength as them.

When young girls drink alcohol or smoke marijuana they are easily tempted into sexual encounters with the opposite sex at an age when they are simply too young to cope with such intense physical intimacy. This is rarely the sort of sex they've been dreaming about. Where are the fireworks? Where is the passion? In her pain and disillusion, probably ill and jaded from the effects of the drug she has used, a young girl is left feeling only that she has lost something precious to herself. Sadly, many girls blame themselves. Wondering why they didn't like sex after all, wishing they hadn't done it, longing for the security of their girlfriends' company, some of them become convinced they are gay. Others just resign themselves to the certainty that there must be something badly wrong with them.

In Jake's story he talks about his 'best friend', Ria, who was fifteen and stoned when they first had sex and continued to use drugs while they 'tried it in all positions' over the next two years. Later she seemed unreasonably upset when he devoted himself to another girl at a party. Then, on the last day of school and apparently without any warning, Ria 'burst into tears' and told him she thought she might be a lesbian. 'So that was the end of our sexual relationship.'

Poor Ria.

Sex, drugs and rock'n'roll? Stick to the music. All you'll hurt is your ears. And maybe you'll get famous. Sex and drugs won't take you anywhere but down.

In this chapter, information on sex and drugs was provided by Dr Alvera Stern, who visited Sydney in 1998 as a guest of Drug Watch Australia. Dr Stern is a director of Macro International Inc.; she works on US Government contracts in the area of substance abuse and has spent thirty years in alcohol, tobacco and other drug abuse prevention activities.

Ben nodded politely at Lucy at school and sometimes half waved, but he didn't try to speak to her for a whole week. The other girls noticed, of course, and came to ask her what had happened. She shrugged. 'I suppose he wasn't worth having,' said Rebecca. They all assumed, without her saying a word, that he must have come on to her and that she had brushed him off. In fact, Lucy rather suspected it had been the other way around.

The following weekend he went camping with the guys. Ben's dad thought it would be fun if they tried to remember all their scouting skills. 'There's no challenge in camping in summer,' he said. 'Winter's the real test.' He insisted on going along with them but luckily he had his own tent and retired early, with about half a tonne of Mum's secondhand doonas that he'd brought from home.

Ben, Tom and Ritchie sat in their sleeping bags around the fire and talked. The sky was black as fresh tar and there seemed to be a million more stars here in the bush than there were in the city. Ben's head felt clear for the first time in a week. He told his mates what had happened on the beach.

'My dick was the size of a tent pole,' he said. 'I thought I was going to explode. I was scared shitless I would come in my pants.'

'Always boasting,' said Tom, when his mates stopped laughing.

'Anyway,' said Ritchie, 'it was her fault. She gave you a tonguie. What did she expect?'

'Not what she got,' hooted Tom and cacked himself again.

'Seriously?' said Ben. 'You think that's what she wanted? You think she was telling me she wanted – you know – sex?'

'Course she was, ya silly nong,' said Tom. 'She was letting you know you can make the moves. It's time to get rid of it, Ben. It's time to become a man, my man.'

'Yeah, but I just didn't think she would be that sort of girl,' murmured Ben.

'What sort of girl?' said Ritchie, suddenly quite serious. 'Just because a girl wants to have sex with you doesn't mean she's a slut. Girls have their physical needs too, you know, just like us.'

The other two stared at him. 'Since when are you the psychologist?' chortled Tom.

'At least girls don't get hard-ons,' said Ben miserably.

'No, but they get wet, Bennie Boy. Down there in their panties. She wants more than your tongue in her mouth . . .'

'No!' shouted Ben. He got up. 'Shut up Tom! I don't want you talking about Lucy like that.'

Ritchie looked up at his friend.

'If you love her,' said Ritchie, scratching patterns in the dirt, 'it makes everything okay.'

Tom burst out laughing. 'What a load of bullshit!' he bellowed. 'What soap opera are you living in, you GIRL?'

KIM'S STORY

Thirty-eight years ago, Kim's father came to Australia from Malaysia on a boat, the youngest of four brothers and the only son lucky enough to be sent away to make a new life in a free land. He drove taxi cabs to put himself through university but found time to quietly gate crash some of the rich kids' parties where he met a vivacious medical student with a wide smile and a mop of auburn curls. She eventually surprised him by becoming his wife and giving him three sons and a daughter of his own.

Physically at least, Kim at nineteen is his father's boy. He has a narrow, fine-boned face, slanting eyes set wide and shaped like tear drops and a long stream of black hair, tied loosely back in an ebony tail. Only his mouth – wide, warm and generous – is inherited from his mother. His body is lean and he has an exotic almost waif-like quality which is at once both contradictory and appealing. Sinking into a flowery couch, he curls up like a cat and stretches, when he needs to, with the feline power of a young panther.

'I always get on better with females than males. When I was younger my father and I were very close – we went to the park together, we rode bikes, all that sort of thing. Then in high school he became very remote. It got harder and harder to be personal with him. My older brothers have told me it was the same with them. He has trouble coping with his kids' adolescence I think – or maybe there's something else there that I don't yet understand about him. He seems to be a lonely man.

My brothers are a lot older than me and they were not

around much while I was growing up. The next one up from me is my sister Joy and she is very tolerant of me and we talk quite a lot, although not so much since she has been married. I'm very close to my mother. She always worked only part-time in her clinic so she could be around for us. She is the one who brought us up. I tell her almost everything. Almost. Not so much since I've been at university. Anyway, I think there has always been a strong female influence on my life.

I'm in my third year of science at university. It's expected of us that we do well academically. I worked hard at school and did well enough – perhaps not well enough to please my father. I have always loved arts, but you know – it's a bit cumbersome to study those subjects. This way I can still leave the door open – I might even be a doctor after all, one day.

I still live at home, but being the youngest I have a fair amount of freedom. I'm enjoying my life now very much. The future is full of all sorts of possibilities.

I remember some time during my first two years at school, comparing genitals with my best friend. Even back then I was always in love with some girl. My one true love in primary school was very flamboyant – she really talked to you, whereas most kids that age said they were "going out" with people but never actually spoke to them.

I went to a Life Education class in Year Six, when I was eleven. I wasn't shocked – being the youngest, I had seen a bit of what had happened to the others. The information they gave us just put everything into perspective. I found out how girls' bodies worked, which was something I hadn't known about before. Well, I knew a couple of girls in the grade had started their periods, because the rumours spread like wildfire when that sort of thing happened. It was interesting to me that someone our age was changing from just being a girl at school into a sexual being – that her chest would stop being flat, that she would start looking a bit like the models and movie stars we all admired.

I received all the correct information I needed about sexuality. We were updated during high school. When it came to separating the information from the reality it was a little harder, of course, but I've always known what I have to know.

I think I always wanted to have girlfriends because I was brought up on romance – we used to watch black-and-white movies, Cathy and Heathcliff, *Pride and Prejudice*, Laurence Olivier classics – all that romance and hidden passion. I think I've always been more interested in the romantic stuff rather than the sex.

I had a girlfriend as soon as I started high school. She was a bit of a strutter – people noticed her – but actually we only ever talked. The first proper girlfriend I had was Terri. She and this guy, Gary, were a couple when we were all in Year Eight. They would walk around the playground holding hands and sometimes they'd kiss. I remember thinking: "Oh wow! People actually do this." Luckily for me, Gary and his family moved overseas and by the end of the year Terri had realised she had quite a thing for me. I certainly had a thing for her. So we started going out – well we actually only went out once, as we were only about thirteen, but you know, we hung out together and we talked on the phone all the time.

She was the first girl I kissed. We were at her house and another couple from our grade were there but I wasn't even aware of them. I was concentrating. It took a lot of courage to do that first kiss. I mean, we had snuggled and been close but when you're thirteen and it's your first time, it still takes a lot of concentration to get around to the actual kissing. We managed three kisses, nice ones.

We went out for about eleven months. My parents knew about us. They had no problem with it which annoyed Joy, my sister, because she'd had a horrible time with having boyfriends, because our father kept such a close watch on her. They were much more lenient with me. Perhaps they thought that being the youngest, I wasn't old enough to get up to anything. It was a family joke that I was going out with a girl who never spoke. She was quite shy around my parents. But actually, we talked a lot when we were by ourselves.

We would go into my room and shut the door. We would make out – touching each other's bodies, exploring, feeling each other. We never actually exposed our bodies ... but we were pretty enthralled with each other. Each time we had the opportunity of doing this we went a little further and a little further.

Mum told me we shouldn't be shutting ourselves up like that. She said it wasn't a good idea. There was this rule that we were never supposed to be totally alone together, like, not in the house when nobody else was home. But Mum wasn't always there.

One afternoon after the athletics carnival, Terri came home with me and we were both aware that we wanted it to happen. We had turned fourteen by then. We'd been talking about it, we were sure it would happen that day. I had condoms ready but I was very tentative with her, because it was going to be the first time for both of us. She was very nervous. We were on my bed and it was all going very well, we were taking our clothes off at last.

Then the phone rang. It really killed the mood. I'd been so excited, I was actually quite shocked that it all stopped so suddenly.

The terrible thing for me was that it didn't happen at all after that. Terri was quite scared by the whole experience and she decided she didn't want sex any more.

It was vexing for me – such a wasted opportunity.

We kept going out until the end of that year but one day, quite unexpectedly, she rang me and said she wanted to finish it because it was all getting too physical.

I was absolutely crushed. For about two months I was an absolute mess. I felt I had lost someone I really cared about. Not long after we broke up, Gary came back and they became a couple again and they stayed together for about five years. It could have given me a complex, I suppose, but it didn't.

I noticed in the change rooms that I was one of the first in my grade to get hair under my arms but my voice got deeper very slowly. Puberty wasn't a big deal for me. I masturbated – it's just a natural part of life, isn't it?

My parents *never* discussed sex with me. I'm not sure why. They are doctors after all. It has just never been mentioned. I vaguely remember having showers with my father when I was very small, but that's all. My mother has a complex about how she looks so there has never been any nudity on display at home. None. In fact I have never thought of my parents as physical beings. If you can't see it, it doesn't exist.

After Terri and I had been going out for a while, John, my sister's husband once said to me: 'You do know about safe sex, don't you?' I was a little embarrassed although he was very relaxed about it, he's a very easy going guy. I think he had this idea that young boys, you know, weren't responsible. I told him I was okay, but it was nice to know that somebody in the family was prepared to talk to me about it if I wanted to.

When I went back to school in Year Ten I noticed a couple of beautiful girls I hadn't talked to before, because of Terri. There was some chat, and some snuggling and kissing but after a while I realised I didn't want to go out with either of them; I wasn't emotionally involved and that's important to me.

I was desperate to be in a relationship again because I had been so happy with Terri, but it takes more than physical stuff to make a real relationship.

I spent most of my sixteenth year with mates. It's always been easy for me to get with girls but that year I hung out with other guys. I'm not really a blokey sort of person but it was good. I was in a band – I play guitar, drums and piano. We used to jam. I started smoking dope about that time. We talked about all sorts of things but we didn't discuss girls much. To talk about girls and sex is pretty degrading for the girls in question. It's not something I would do.

I wasn't concerned about my virginity. I've always turned my nose up at the idea of the one night stand. What I've always liked is the idea of having a romantic relationship with one person. If two people love each other and really care about each other, I believe sex will naturally follow when they are ready.

I was about seventeen when I became friendly with Prue. She was in my drama class, a real bookworm, she reminded me a lot of my sister. We were opposites and at first she got on my nerves. But she pursued me fairly actively which was a nice change. We went out for a few months but I took my time with her because I didn't want to make the same mistake I had made with Terri. We did some kissing and some touching but we weren't very adventurous – we didn't actually see each other that much because by Year Eleven we were both pretty busy with study.

Then this new girl called Ashleigh arrived at the school. She was just a bit shorter than me, a large-boned girl with a full bosom, long, light brown hair and wonderful eyes. Gorgeous. We discovered we had a lot in common, like our views on politics and society and we liked the same music. We talked for hours and we became really good friends. Prue and I broke up while I was getting to know Ashleigh.

Ashleigh lived two streets away from me and I began seeing her every day. She was my best friend – she still is. Even back then, though, it was a friendship rather than a romance.

By then my parents had given up the "you can't be alone with them" thing and we had a lot more freedom to be together. Ashleigh was as keen as I was to explore the physical side of things. We took our clothes off and lay on her bed; we had a few false starts at intercourse and the first time we actually managed penetration, we didn't use protection. I didn't ejaculate – it was sort of weird. I wasn't in love, the way I had expected to be. I think she felt more strongly about me than I did about her. But we were very close and we cared about each other very much.

It wasn't what I expected. It wasn't romantic, like in the movies. To find someone you are really truly madly deeply in love with is hard. Having sex with Ashleigh just wasn't a *Wuthering Heights* sort of thing.

Physically it worked well. It was her first time, so we learned together. Well, we couldn't keep away from each other. Ashleigh had to keep sending her mother out of the house. I used to smoke dope before we had sex, although Ashleigh didn't. It wasn't because I needed drugs to enhance the experience – it was just habit. We used condoms – I was sort of worried about that because I thought it would be awkward but it wasn't ever a problem. Then Ashleigh went on the pill.

At school, despite the sexual developments, it was surprisingly comfortable to be around Ashleigh. We remained best friends. About halfway through our final year at school, when we had been having a very intense sexual relationship for about seven months, I told her I wanted to break up. We were just so comfortable with each other. Even the sex was getting comfortable and sort of ordinary. I couldn't handle having a physical relationship with someone who was my closest mate, if you know what I mean. She agreed, although I don't think she really understood. She still really liked me.

After that we missed the sexual side of things – we were a bit frustrated – but we were still really comfortable in each other's company.

Now this is a bit embarrassing and with hindsight, I wouldn't do this again, but I had been a peer support leader in Year Eleven and one of the young girls I was in charge of had a bit of a crush on me. Her name was Kate and she was only thirteen. On the other hand she was tall and she had very long blonde hair. She was very mature for her age. We became quite close.

There was nothing secret about our friendship and some of the guys in her grade made some snide and racist remarks about what I was doing with her. I also got some ribbing from my own friends. But I still believed that the only thing that mattered in a relationship was that you were both sincere and really cared about each other.

I had my licence by then and I would borrow the car and go to see her at weekends. There was a lot of – I think they call it outercourse. I made it to every base but home. But I never forced anything on her. Towards the end she was ready for it, I think, but by then I had lost interest.

My mother was concerned about my friendship with Kate. She made her very welcome at our house but she didn't think what I was doing was wise. We were coming up to final exams at the time and she was very supportive of me, cutting back her hours so she could be around while I was sitting for the big one.

My father wasn't too pleased with me for other reasons. He didn't think I was working hard enough. I don't study hard but I knew I could do better than he expected and as it turned out, I was right.

After the HSC I had a wonderful summer. Through a friend of mine I met Hayley. She was the most beautiful girl I had ever seen in my life. She had a lovely face and these long, long legs...and she was only fourteen years old. She was as tall as a model and you wouldn't have guessed her age. The first night I met her was the closest I had ever come to a one night fling. But she had a wicked stepfather who was obsessed with protecting his little girl and he warned me off like death.

We did go out, but it was difficult to be alone. After a couple of months I realised it wasn't working. We had very little to say to each other. She was very self-righteous. Even though she was so young, she thought she knew everything. Also I found out she had been coming on really strong to another guy during Christmas Carols in the Domain. It was the first time I had ever been treated badly by a girl but it wasn't surprising. She knew she was beautiful and she used it like nothing else; she was a terrible flirt.

I had a great summer. I had the use of my sister's car and I could drive anywhere and go any place. Then Ashleigh and I started university. She was still my best friend. We developed this game where we would just lie on the grass together, watching the people passing by, and we would pick out people we thought we should be attracted to. I had my eye on a girl who always wore T-shirts from bands I liked. So one day I went up to her and said: "Nice shirt" and after that we started talking and getting together from time to time. Her name was Lou. One day we were sitting on the lawn in front of the uni and she leaned over and kissed me.

I went home and wrote her a long long letter about what I was looking for in a relationship. I tend to be a bit wordy and I think it really scared her off. She told me it was nothing personal but she wasn't ready for anything so intense at that time of her life.

Ashleigh and I started playing our stalking game again and we targeted Karen, who Ashleigh said was "my type". I was a bit alarmed when I realised that all the girls who were supposed to be "my type" were small and fine-boned and dark-haired – in other words, they looked very much like my sister. So I was determined to find a girl who wasn't "my type" at all. Eventually I spotted Rachel, who was tall and curvaceous, with fair skin and thick, light-brown curls and I watched her for quite a while.

People tell me I am different to other guys. A lot of girls confide things to me that they wouldn't tell other blokes. I was let in on a 'deep and meaningful' conversation at a girls' party once and I was quite shocked at how open they are – quite different to guys.'

Kim speaks about the girls he has known with a faraway, dreamy look on his exotic face. But when the subject of his family arises again he leans forward, clasps his hands, sighs and looks anxious.

'It really is very hard to get on with my father, you see. And my brothers are so much older. My mother gets quite distraught trying to communicate with my father. She has threatened to leave him because he won't – you know – open up. My mother is very warm, very open. Of course she wouldn't leave – she cares too much. But it's hard for her.

Last year I went for a holiday to China with my father which was an interesting experience as we hadn't had the experience of being that close since I was a child. We survived the two weeks without killing each other, but I don't know if we became closer – because nobody else spoke English, we were forced to find something in common, to have something to talk about. My father is a fourth-generation Chinese but he had never actually been to China and he doesn't speak Chinese.

When I returned to university I concentrated on Rachel, who I kept seeing at lectures and at the bar. I was determined to speak to her so I went up to her and said: "nice shirt". Well, it had worked the previous time and I was wearing the same one, so it was an attempt at wit. Anyway, it didn't work – it's hard to just go up to someone at uni and have a conversation about nothing.

Finally, a few weeks later, Rachel was with a guy I knew and we ended up talking for hours. Eventually I told her I had a crush on her and she was taken aback. She told me she couldn't go out with me as she was a religious person and she wouldn't go out with anyone who wasn't the same religion as she was.

That was okay, we continued to just chat when we saw each other. Then one weekend, Ashleigh and some friends decided to rent a house up the coast and they invited Rachel to come too.

During the night she came and lay down on a mattress beside me and we started kissing. Then she began to tell me things about herself – she said she actually was interested in me, but she was still recovering from a very traumatic period in her life. She had been raped two years earlier. She'd had a boyfriend who had beaten her up. As a result she had a problem getting it on with guys. She said she knew I was too nice a guy to hurt her. So we kissed some more and then we went to sleep.

The next day everyone else went home and only Rachel and I were left. That night we smoked a bit of dope and then we had sex together. The trouble is, because I hadn't been expecting anything like that to happen, I didn't have any condoms. She said everything would be okay. I asked her if we would now be able to see each other regularly but she said she still wasn't sure she could handle a relationship.

We started going out, just as friends. Her parents were very strict and we never slept together again – there was no physical contact whatsoever. The whole thing was becoming very strained while she tried to make up her mind about whether she could face having a relationship with me after everything she had already been through.

Ever since I broke up with my very first girlfriend, Terri, I had never felt so strongly about a girl. I had been looking for romance for so long and when Rachel came along I felt the same tingles, the same feelings.

One night Rachel told me that after our single night of sex up the coast, she had become pregnant. She had decided to have an abortion but had suffered a miscarriage a few weeks later.

It must have been horrible for her. In her place I'd have been absolutely terrified. It took me a long time to get over the shock. I felt. . .I became really depressed.

It's hard to be sort of hanging around in limbo. I know I have never had anything like the problems she's experienced. I know none of the guys she has ever been with have lasted longer than a few weeks. It's difficult convincing her that our relationship could work. But even without touching her, I am happy to be around her, I am content just to be with her.

I don't know if Rachel is *the* one. We haven't known each other long enough for that. We're seeing each other regularly and I'd like to think this is a relationship that will grow. We've only slept together that one time. Since she told me what happened I have practically sworn myself to celibacy. It was pretty scary.

Through all this, Ashleigh has still remained my best friend. She has not had a proper boyfriend since we broke up but she's never been jealous of my girlfriends. My Mum often says: "What about poor old Ashleigh?" but I don't think of her that way. I have had male friends but none of them have ever been as close to me as Ashleigh. I try to see her every day and we still talk about anything and everything. But we are friends, not lovers. I could probably sleep in the same bed as Ashleigh and we still wouldn't have sex.

I still want to be in love. I want it to be really wonderful. I think I am a lot more willing to work at a relationship than many other people my age. I want something that really means everything to me and to the person I love and I want it to stay that way forever.'

A LITTLE BIT PREGNANT: WHAT'S HAPPENING, BABY?

In reality, sexual intercourse is designed purely for procreation – for making new people. Because we are human beings and well advanced on the evolutionary scale, we also have the luxury, and perhaps the pain, of choosing to have sex for other reasons.

But putting aside passion, lust and fun, the main item on the sexual agenda is now, has been and always will be – making babies.

HOW BABIES GET STARTED

To make a baby you need an egg, which comes from the female, and a sperm, which comes from the male, and you also need the conditions that make it possible for this egg and this sperm to meet and fuse together in the female's body.

Forget about choices. Everything in a man's body and a woman's body is geared up to make this happen. From the time a girl starts getting her period and a boy starts making sperm, as far as nature is concerned and whether they like it or not, she's a woman and he's a man and they are capable of making babies.

Every month in a woman's body, an egg is produced in either one of her two ovaries. The egg travels out of the ovary, and down the Fallopian tube towards the uterus.

If she has sexual intercourse with a male during this time, the egg, which is on its way down, can meet the sperm, which is on its way up. In most cases there is only one egg, but there are a lot of sperm, all swimming like mad in their race to do what a man's got to do!

For the egg to be fertilised, some pretty ideal conditions are involved. Generally it works best when the penis has been fully inserted into the vagina. The sperm is spurted out and drawn up through the cervix, which is the opening to the uterus or womb; the sperm continues to swim up into the Fallopian tubes. One lucky sperm wins the race, finds its way to the egg in the Fallopian tube and fuses with the egg. The now-fertilised egg then continues its journey down through the Fallopian tube into the uterus where it attaches itself to the wall and begins to grow. It takes about ten days for all this to happen.

Sometimes, depending on what stage the woman's periodic cycle has reached, the egg gets all the way down into the uterus before it meets up with the sperm. Fertilisation can still take place in the uterus, although the chances of this happening are reduced.

The egg begins to grow – and grow – and grow – into a baby. The uterus (womb) is like an oven in which the baby is formed and baked, hopefully to perfection. There are many excellent books which describe in detailed words and pictures how a baby is made. Some are listed on page 250.

TEENAGE PREGNANCY

No matter how much we learn about eggs and sperm and fertilisation, the creation of a new human life is a miracle. Part of it will always remain a mystery. Nobody really understands what complex and incredible forces combine within a woman's body to make it possible for her to have a baby.

When a teenage girl discovers she is pregnant, miracles are generally the furthest thing from her mind. If she has had sex without protection and her period fails to come, she is almost always gripped by fear and anxiety. And a faint, horrified sense of disbelief ...

I don't know whether you're there at all.

But the thought that you might be there is like a drip, drip, drip that won't go away, day and night, day and night ...

like a clock that never stops ticking.

Pregnant, pregnant, what if I'm pregnant? Tick tock tick tock tick ...

I'm so frightened at night that I can hardly breathe.

I can't tell anyone ... I can't tell Mum.

You're only a shadow. You're only a whisper ...

Leave me alone.

I don't want you.

Go away. Please, please, go away.

(From Dear Nobody, *by Berlie Doherty)*

To be having a baby when you are young and unmarried, when you are still at school or only just beginning your adult life, can seem like a tragedy for many young women. Even though our society no longer spurns 'unwed mothers', teenage girls are understandably frightened when they discover they are pregnant. As much as she might love the young man who fathered the child (and she may not), and despite the support of her family, a young woman is faced with a crisis which will almost certainly change her life and future.

Some adults describe teenage mothers as 'babies having babies'. Of course, adolescent girls are *not* babies, they are growing up fast, becoming independent, learning how to make decisions about their lives and realising that they will have to take responsibility for those decisions. On the other hand, babies steal away the time young men and women need to complete their own development, to have the fun and freedom all adolescents deserve.

Babies need continuous care twenty-four hours a day, seven days a week, 365 days a year. When you are responsible for an infant, there are no holidays, no meal breaks, no nice neat predictable routines. Babies cry a lot, and they poo and wee and are constantly hungry or won't eat at all, which is a dreadful worry. It's the same with their sleeping. Some do, some don't and too much of either causes stress and anxiety. Babies need food and clothing, lots of loving and years of supervision. And they don't stay babies. Within a couple of years they develop an enormous range of needs – from health and hygiene to education. They learn to walk and then they start to run. They need dental care, medical treatment, more and more food, new clothes, transport, swimming lessons. They are expensive.

Taking precautions against unwanted pregnancy during adolescence is a healthy, intelligent and admirable thing to do. Everyone benefits when parenthood is postponed until a young couple are prepared emotionally and financially for the responsibility of parenthood. That's when babies will bring them more love and joy than they ever imagined.

PREGNANCY CHOICES

A pregnant girl can decide to keep and care for her baby herself or with the help of her family. The other two options are adoption or termination of the pregnancy.

ADOPTION

Adoption is a legal process where the newborn baby is put in the care of a couple who have applied to become the legal parents of a child. The selected couple will have been thoroughly investigated by the adoption agency concerned, to ensure that they will make suitable parents. Often, but not always, they are people who have been unable to conceive a child of their own, and who have been yearning to have a family for a long time. Adoption agencies are operated by the state governments and by major church organisations.

There is a lot to find out about adopting out a baby, including whether or not the natural mother wishes to meet the adoptive parents and to be kept informed of the baby's progress through life. The boy who fathered the baby also has legal rights, which must be considered. It's very important for young women to speak with a social worker early in their pregnancy, and to have all these matters explained to them, so that they have time to think carefully about adoption.

TERMINATION OF PREGNANCY (ABORTION)

To bring about the end of a pregnancy, even when it has hardly begun, is a sad and very difficult choice for any woman to make. There has always been much debate about when a baby growing within the uterus (the foetus) actually becomes a living human being. Many people believe an unborn child has the right to life and that no other person has the right to bring an end to that life. Others argue that if the birth of an unplanned and unwanted baby threatens the psychological, emotional and possibly even the physical health of the mother (and perhaps in the long term puts the baby in danger as well), then termination of the pregnancy should be considered.

The question of whether abortion is legal or not is a complicated one. The law relating to abortion varies from state to state and many people believe the laws should be clearer and more liberal. When it comes to terminating pregnancies in girls who are under sixteen, which is the legal age of consent to sex, the law becomes even more complex. Regulations concerning the age of the mother and the stage at which her pregnancy can be legally terminated vary from state to state.

In most states and territories, terminations can be carried out by qualified medical practitioners in approved hospitals and clinics, providing the doctor or doctors who have been consulted believe the pregnancy puts the physical or mental health of the mother at risk.

Teenage girls need to think about abortion very carefully, taking into account their own moral and religious beliefs and how this decision might affect their lives in the future. The best thing to do is talk to a doctor or a social worker, to find out what is involved. They should also discuss the problem with their parents, or if this is out of the question, with an understanding adult relative, a minister of religion if they know one, or a counsellor at a family planning clinic or a public hospital. Most hospitals have people who are specially trained to advise adolescents.

Ideally, the girl should consult the father of her unborn baby as well. Whether this is possible will depend on her relationship with him and the degree of interest and support he has shown in relation to her pregnancy.

HOW A PREGNANCY IS TERMINATED

A termination involves removing the tiny foetus and placenta from the young woman's uterus. How this is done depends on how far pregnant she is. It's best if a termination is carried out within the first three months of pregnancy. This should takes place in a hospital or special clinic.

Before the procedure, the girl is given either a local anaesthetic or a sedative and occasionally a general anaesthetic to put her to sleep. A very thin plastic tube called a catheter is then inserted into her uterus and the contents are sucked out. The contents resemble bright red blood.

Most women have some bleeding and a few cramps afterwards. This feels like period pain. They should rest and take special care of their health for a week or two after the operation.

If the pregnancy is more advanced than twelve weeks, a more complicated operation is necessary.

HELEN'S STORY

The difficulty, when listening to her story, is reconciling the purity and beauty of Helen's face with the horrors of all that she's experienced in her seventeen years in the outer suburbs of the city's west.

She is a tall girl with crisp, deep auburn hair, pulled severely back and wound into a long, thick plait which hangs down her very straight back. Her perfect skin is alabaster; her brown eyes dance and sparkle when she laughs, which is often. She has a generous mouth and beautiful white, even teeth. Her grey pants and a loose grey wool smock almost hide the swell of her belly; she moves gracefully around the scrupulously clean but dingy front room of the Housing Commission home she shares with her mother, her husband and her small blond son.

Helen's voice is deep and musical. She should be in the movies, up on the big screen, singing country and western ballads while the audience sighs at her loveliness and her heartbreak. But make-up or lighting could not make her more beautiful than she is in the fifth month of her second pregnancy, and despite the sadness of her story, there is no sign of despair.

'Mum and Dad got married when I was four. I was the flowergirl at the wedding. Mum was pregnant and they loved each other but Dad was always drinking and gambling away their money for the rent. They were always fighting and then Mum would start drinking as well. My brother, Michael, was born ill because of that – there were medical complications and he had to stay in hospital for a long time. That made it even harder for Mum.

When I was six she decided to leave my father and we ended up in a refuge. She applied for a commission house and we got one out this way. We didn't care where it was, as long as we could live a more settled life. We lived there until I was thirteen.

My earliest memories of anything sexual are when I was about six and my friend's stepfather showed me his penis. I didn't know what was going on and neither did my friend. He had sex toys and he told us to try them out. I can't remember much about it, except that it wasn't very nice. There was never any intercourse or penetration thank bloody goodness. My friend dobbed him in but before anything happened about it he went and shot himself. What a silly arsehole!

When we were settled in our new house, Dad found us and Mum took him back but the same thing started happening – he was drinking and hitting her – so she threw him out again. She stopped the drink herself and those were the best years of my life, when Mum was off the grog and Dad came to take us out on Sundays and always brought lollies. Mum used to have a good job in a big store in the city, until she started drinking again. After that she mainly just got some barmaid work.

Mum and Dad got divorced and unfortunately she took up with this complete loser. Nathan his name was. Telling Mum she was mad to have him was like talking to a brick wall. He was with us for six years. At first he wasn't too bad, he seemed like a caring person – he was nice to Mum and he had time to spend with Michael and me to do things that Dad never did – but after a while, when he noticed

Mum was paying us more attention than him, he started getting more aggressive to her. She never used to say anything, she never went to the police station and reported him. The beatings got more and more frequent. It was all because of us. When Michael and I didn't do what Nathan wanted, Mum would cop it. She started drinking again and he couldn't handle that so he started drinking and taking drugs. Mum wasn't into the drugs as far as I know.

She finally reported him, but the silly woman, you know, she'd ring the police and they'd come out and she'd say: "Oh well, he said he wouldn't do it again." All the usual excuses. And the police say: "Well we can't do anything about it unless you lay formal charges." But she didn't. So after a while they started taking their time about coming out because they knew it would always be the same.

One day she finally did charge him and they took him away in a paddy wagon – two hours later, he was back again. I couldn't believe it. She wouldn't let him in, so he went under the house and stayed there and knew where we were and what we were doing from our footsteps on the floor above his head. The next day he says he just wants a shower and then he'll leave. Of course Mum, being the silly woman that she is, lets him in. He has a shower and gets changed and then he gets his mouth going: "It'll never happen again, blah blah blah" – and he stays.

Then he started picking on me, pretty much. Before long I started copping the beatings as well as Mum. He put me in hospital once – I was putting something in the bin and he came along and took a flying kick at me and I wasn't fast enough to get away from him and he broke my fingers. He's done the whole kit and caboodle with me. Slapped my face.

Punched me in the ribs. Fractured a rib in fact. After a while you think to yourself: "Why should I put up with this? Mum might be willing to, but I'm not."

By then I was about twelve, but I vaguely remembered what it had been like when Mum and Dad were together and that hadn't been a very nice environment for a child either. Now with this Nathan around, I thought I could well end up lying there dead. So could Mum. I told her that many times but he always threatened her that if she left him he'd kill us.

So I went and told my teacher. I was in the last year of primary school. I was school captain. Of course, once I'd told them what was happening at home, that was the end of all that sort of thing.

My teacher already knew something was wrong. He called in DOCS (Department of Community Services) and in a way it turned out to be the worst mistake of my life because they didn't do anything about Nathan, but they took me away from my Mum and put me in foster home after foster home. The thing is, I still loved my mum even though I was angry at her because she wanted to stay with Nathan. The way I looked at it at the time, she had chosen him over me. But that wasn't really the case, because she was copping it every night while I was safe, at least. She had just been trying to protect us.

The first foster home had a family of three and they were quite nice but it was only a short-term stay so then they sent me to a church place for homeless girls. It was about that time that I first got my periods and I was still only twelve. At first I was completely freaked out. I thought:

"Oh my *God* ! What's *that*?" I mean, I knew what it was because my mum had told me all about it, but I was shocked because I wasn't ready – I didn't think it was time. But I asked the lady at the home and she told me everything Mum had already told me and helped me get fixed up with what I needed.

Mum had pretty well prepared me for that sort of thing. In that way she was a very practical woman – she made sure I knew everything I had to. From quite early on my mother was always saying to me: "When you're ready to have sex, tell me and we'll put you on the pill so you don't go and have a baby when you're so young." But did I listen? Did I pay attention to my mother? *No! No! No!* And look at where it got me now!

I quite liked it at the girls' home and I stayed for a year. But they thought it would be better for me if a relative could take me. After some more court appearances I was sent to live with my stepbrother and his partner – my dad had two sons from before he married Mum. John and I got on all right as brother and sister but as a father-figure he was very strict, especially about the education and learning stuff. I was a teenager by then and I was getting a bit rebellious so I would tell John to "get mmphed", you know, excuse the language. And Dad was always coming around telling him to leave me alone because I was just a kid and I shouldn't have to study. But in a way I'm glad now that John made me do that study because otherwise I wouldn't have learned as much as I did – not that I know much because I didn't end up finishing school anyway.

They were expecting their first child so we went back to court and I ended up living with my other stepbrother,

Peter, and his wife and son. I had always really liked visiting them but living with their problems as well as my own was too hard so I decided to run away. I saved up the money Dad had given me and my lunch money and one day I didn't go to school – I went back to Mum's.

I hadn't seen Mum properly for ages – all our access visits had been supervised and we couldn't go out together. Everything was taped and monitored, we couldn't go and get Maccas or sit in the park and talk properly or anything.

Peter rang the police and they turned up at Mum's and I told them all I wanted to do was be with my mother. I ended up in the home for girls again. And that's where I met up with Joanna.

Well, we were the most rebellious teenagers you could ever imagine. We got up to naughty tricks. We went to different high schools but we'd meet and wag it every day. One day they followed us and found out what we were doing and they threatened to throw us out of there. I thought: "Oh wonderful!" I rang Mum and told her what was happening and she was pretty cranky at me. She said: "What are you doing, ruining your life, you know you can do so well at school."

I had been doing quite well but I had been to a few of them by then and after a while you get so sick and tired of changing schools all the time. You have to keep making new friends and you have to keep adapting to every new school method and all the different rules. Anyway, at the last school I went to they didn't give a damn about you. So why bother going?

Anyway, Nathan had gone to gaol so the courts said I was allowed to go home to Mum. It was the best day!

I agreed to go to school and make a bit of an effort. But I asked her if Joanna could come and stay as well and she said yes, as long as she was willing to help out and that. I think that was the biggest mistake Mum ever made! She thought we were really good friends – and we were – but she lived to regret that decision.'

At this stage, and not for the first time, Helen stops talking and convulses with laughter. After hugging herself with glee and giggling for a while, she resumes her tale.

'We met these guys, total losers in a way. Jo ended up going out with Jeff and I had the other one, Matty, and they had the drugs, so we got into the drugs too. They had dope and they did a bit of speed and other stuff. I smoked dope, but not the other stuff – I never wanted to be whacked off my face, I had seen what it does to you. I never drank – not after seeing what it did to Mum and Dad.

I was smoking pot very regularly though, pretty much every day, yeah. If Matty didn't have any I could always get a quick fix from my stepbrother, Peter, because he had moved and didn't live too far away. So I was pretty dopey a lot of the time, and I wasn't eating properly so I was often quite sick and I lost a lot of weight. Matty was always putting the pressure on me to have sex but I told him he'd have to wait. I was spending a lot of time whacked out of my brain but I still wasn't willing to give up my virginity to this idiot.

The four of us hung out together for six or seven months. Matty's mum was really nice. I used to go to his place just to see her. She'd been pretty much through what my mum had been through and I could relate to her. We'd talk for hours and then Matty would come in, off his face, and I'd think: "What am I doing? Am I crazy?"

When I finally had enough I broke it off. He was treating me like a piece of crud, pretty much, and I felt I deserved better. I felt quite upset about it – this was the first real relationship with a boy that I had ever had and in the beginning he was okay. I was more into the idea of being "in love" with someone, really, but the problem was that I didn't actually *like* him.

The thing is, girls of fourteen like to have a boyfriend. You feel left out if you don't have one.

Jo still hadn't had anything sexual happen to her either – not even with Jeff, although they had been together for ages. He didn't want her for the sex. Obviously he must have loved her or something.

Even though I had broken off with Matty I was still hanging out with Jo and Jeff and he had this older brother, Danny, who was about twenty-two. We used to watch him play footy. One day we went to his place and smoked a lot of dope and Jo and Jeff eventually left and you know . . . one thing led to another, and it happened.

I was so high I don't remember anything about it, whether it was painful, what we did, nothing. When I woke up the next morning I didn't have a clue where I was. You wake up and you think: "What have I done?" And he walks in and gives you a big smile and you think: "Oh no! Biggest mistake of my life."

I haven't hung out with him or anything since. I mean, we say "hi" but we wouldn't even stop and chat. It was just one of those one night things that went one step further than it should have.

Pretty much because of that I cut down on the marijuana. I didn't ever want to be out of control like that again. I gave up dope in one big hit and it took its toll on me, but I took up smoking normal cigarettes.

Nathan was back with Mum by then and he had stopped beating me up but I was worried about my young brother, Michael, who had been with them all along. Michael never said Nathan had hit him or anything, but there were things, you know. He said he broke his collarbone falling off his bike and I thought: "Oh sure". But then he did fall off his bike and he broke his collarbone again. So how do you know what's the truth? Anyway, I believe Nathan started laying into Michael about that time but then the police caught up with him again.

He went to gaol for three months and during that time I said to Mum: "Do you want to live the rest of your life like this? Do you want to keep on wondering when you're going to cop the next backhand or whether you're going to see the next morning alive?"

She ended up going to domestic violence meetings and things like that and while he was in gaol we moved to this place which is also Housing Commission but it's a fair way from our old suburb.

Not that it made any difference in the end, because when Nathan got out, he found us and he phoned. It was one morning, and I was getting dressed. After a while I heard Mum saying, you know, oh well, he could come over just to talk. So I finished getting dressed for school – I was in Year Eight – and I decided I'd had enough. I told Jo I was shooting through. That meant she didn't have anywhere to stay either, so she came with me.

We had a friend called Kenny who was getting this flat and he said we could stay there as long as we cleaned up after ourselves and whatever.

That was how I met Raymond. I was fourteen, he was eighteen and in his final year of school. He was tall and dark and fairly quiet. He had the use of his parents' car and he came around and picked us up, with our stuff, and we went to Kenny's. He used to come around to Kenny's quite a lot. We talked sometimes but it was very gradual, the way we got to know each other. I mean we didn't talk for hours and hours or anything.

Leaving home that time meant the end of school for me. I never went back after that. I did my share of the cleaning up at Kenny's but Jo was her usual self-serving self and she only did what she felt like. She just sat around staring into space or else she was out with her boyfriend. In the end Kenny threatened to throw us both out, which wasn't very fair on me. It was a pretty hard time for me, having just left my mum and everything. What I didn't know at that stage was that Raymond was going through a hard time with his mum at home – she was having a sort of breakdown – which is why he came around to Kenny's so much.

One night the others all went off to a movie and I didn't feel like it and Raymond didn't want to go either. He stayed home and kept me company. Anyway, somebody came knocking on the door and yelling that they had come to get me. I don't know who it was. It might have been Mum or Dad, because they were worried about where I was, or it might have been DOCS. Raymond and I were watching TV, so we just turned off all the lights and we sat there in the dark together and held our breath and kept deathly quiet.

Whoever it was, they went away. Then Kenny and Jo and Jeff came home. I was supposed to be sharing the second bedroom with Jo but she and Jeff were having sex by this time so when they were sleeping together I would just drag my mattress out of there and sleep in the kitchen. That's what I did on this night as well, only Raymond came and joined me – yeah, on the mattress, on the kitchen floor. Really romantic. Well it was pretty silly that he should sleep on the bare floor when there was some mattress available.

Pretty much one thing led to another. Because I had only had sex that one time before it kind of hurt but I enjoyed it more than the first time. We didn't take any precautions, though.

We were inseparable from then on. His parents were having troubles of their own and he wanted to be out of the house as much as he could. He went home and got his clothes and the stuff that he owned that was worth something and he sold a lot of it, so we had enough money to get away.

The funny thing is, we didn't have sex any more for a couple of months. The first time, on the mattress in the kitchen, had all been very unplanned and very unexpected. I don't even remember much about it. We hadn't actually had a relationship with each other and we needed to experience that before we slept with each other again.

We ended up going to Queensland. The lease had run out on Kenny's flat in any case and we had nowhere to go. Well, Raymond's mum wasn't going to take me in, was she?

We went to Brisbane by coach and we stayed with Raymond's grandparents. They didn't mind but they were on the pension and it was pushing them to the limits having two extra mouths to feed – and, of course, neither of us had jobs.

They put me in their spare bedroom and Raymond slept on a divan in the lounge room. They wouldn't let us sleep together. I was still only fourteen.

Eventually Raymond got a job and we went to live in a caravan. Unfortunately he only got paid on commission so some weeks would be good and other weeks he would hardly make anything.

We came back to Sydney after a couple of months. It had all been too hard. Mum said we could move in with her, here. She said we didn't have to pay for any of the bills or anything until Raymond got a job. She gave us her bed – she went into my old room and slept in my single bed when she was home. So we finally got around to having sex again, but I felt quite embarrassed and awkward at first, even thought I knew it was bound to happen sooner or later.

Mum had a new boyfriend, Teddy, and she spent most of the time; at his place. Mind you, Nathan still rang from time to time, he still does. He rang not so long ago. His latest girlfriend died from a drug overdose. He rings up and wants to talk to me about the past. I said: "The past is past, I don't want to talk about it, I don't want to *reminisce*." He asks for Mum but I just say: "I'll tell her you called."

I knew I was pregnant two weeks before my periods were even due. I rang Mum and told her I was really tired and she said: "I bet you're pregnant."

We'd been having sex regularly for nearly a year by then and we had never taken any precautions and nothing had ever happened so I didn't worry about it too much. I thought I was just lucky. I was actually thinking about going on the pill, but it was too late.

I was happy and I was sad at the same time, because I was so young. Mum was furious at me because I was still only fourteen and she saw it as giving up my life. I agreed with her. It was my fault for being sexually active and not taking precautions. And I'm paying the consequences now. I accept that. I don't believe in abortion, I don't believe in adoption, so this is what has happened. I have little Rhett.

Mum had always been there for me and I never doubted that she still would be. She came around – she wanted to be involved, because it was her grandson, after all. But she was back drinking again and things were getting harder so we ended up moving out and going to live with Raymond's parents. They were more than willing to have us but they expected us to pay our way – rent and board. Raymond had a few jobs, washing cars, working as a salesman, he was always trying hard to find employment. He was on and off the dole.

My Dad was furious. He wanted me to have an abortion or give it up for adoption. I said: "Do not tell me how to run my life, you of all people. If you don't want to be part of this child's life, then don't."

At that stage I had never had a job. I found some part-time work as a checkout chick but I fainted a lot at work and I used to get very tired. Finally, after fainting again, I decided it was a sign that I shouldn't be doing it so I gave it up.

I made plans though. I decided that after I got the new baby settled I would do my school certificate through TAFE, and I thought I could also probably get some part-time work if Raymond and I shared the babysitting.

I ended up going to hospital when I was seven months pregnant because I was bleeding. Dad heard about it and came around and said he was sorry, and he has been a big part of it all since then.

My girlfriend, Joanna, ended up having a baby with her boyfriend, right after she heard about me. But even though they had been going so well, things ended up going badly for them and they're not together any more, but she still has the kid.

Raymond really can't stand Jo. It's one of the few things we don't feel the same about. She was my closest friend for so long and we went through a lot together.

My Mum and I stayed close. I wanted her to be there for the birth, but I sent her home from the hospital at some stage and of course that's when little Rhett decided to come, wasn't it?

I think I'm doing quite well at motherhood, considering I'd never had any other kind of proper job. Raymond's mum took two weeks off work to help me when I first came home from hospital. Looking after Rhett hasn't been a burden, even though I would not normally have done it this early. Fifteen is really too young to be a mum.

We were married when Rhett was sixteen months old. I was seventeen and Raymond was twenty-one. We had to get special permission from the courts because I was underage. The only reason we got married was that his parents had a life insurance policy which they had been paying into for years. When Raymond turned twenty-one they said he could have the money as long as he used it for something special – you know, not just paying the car off or something. So we had a wedding! Everybody came. We had a wonderful time.

Things were looking a lot better for us by then because Raymond had got an engineering apprenticeship. He had regular work at last and he was learning a trade.

I chose Raymond for my husband because he was so different to all the other men in my life. My dad never stuck around. My stepbrothers picked on me. Nathan was no role model for anyone.

From the beginning the only time Raymond and I have been apart was when I was in hospital having Rhett. Oh, and the night before our wedding when we slept apart – to please his mother.

But it was never sex that brought us together. Sex is not the be-all and end-all of a relationship. If Raymond lost his penis I wouldn't be too upset. I would still love him and live with him.

This second pregnancy was a mistake. I was breast-feeding Rhett and the pill I was on was doing bizarre things to my body. When I found out I was pregnant again I was very upset. I so badly want a certificate saying that I have completed school and this means I'll have a lot more trouble getting that.

Raymond lost his job two weeks ago. He got fired because they were cutting back and he was the last one to be taken on. So now he's looking for work again and we are living on my supporting parents' pension which is $356 a fortnight, plus the child allowance of $122. That might sound a lot but by the time you pay for rent and food, there's not much left.

I'd tell any teenage girl who is thinking about getting pregnant just for the sake of it, it is definitely not worth it. You need to buy so much stuff – clothes, formula, nappies – and you're just so busy. You can't get a job and look after a baby and you can't afford child care. There's no way you could be on Cloud Nine with a baby, no way. You'd be silly to do it on purpose.

In the beginning, I liked it that Raymond was someone I could talk to. I knew he wasn't going to hit me, or lead me in the wrong direction. I knew he would look after me. Now I hope we'll stay together forever.

But I'll tell you something. If he ever hurts me, even though we're married, even though we have kids, I'll be gone. I will be out of here.

A lot of people I know who have been through what I've been through don't think life is worth living. They get very depressed, they don't care about anything except using grog or drugs to blank out their past – and their present too, pretty much.

I have a different outlook. I've lived with it all – the problems caused by my parents' rows and drinking, the various breakups in my family, the beatings from Nathan, being shunted from pillar to post by DOCS, the pregnancies – but I've learned from everything that has happened to me. I've decided to just make the best of things.

What else can you do?'

... RAYMOND

While Helen sits bolt upright on the divan and tells her story, Raymond stays in the room, watchful but detached. He sits on the floor, his long legs stretched out, and plays quietly with his sixteen-month-old son, who is seriously involved with an enormous toy tractor, almost the same size as himself.

Raymond is a clean-cut, serious-looking young man; his head is covered with fashionable stubble, there's a token ring in his ear, and

*somehow his owlish glasses seem out of place. He makes no attempt
to interrupt or correct Helen as she speaks, and when asked if it
disturbs him to hear about her sexual history he shrugs and says
he's heard it all before. It almost seems as if he's not listening at all
until he's given the opportunity to speak for himself.*

'Whenever I went around to Kenny's, Helen was there. I had
never thought of her as a person to go out with – it was only
when I knew that she really liked me that I began to feel
differently about her.

I didn't have any condoms with me that night because
I wasn't seeing anyone special at the time and I am not the
sort of person who has one night stands. I always thought I
couldn't have sex with a girl unless I loved her. I didn't love
Helen at the time. It was just something that happened,
with being so physically close that night and after hiding
together and everything. But within a day or two my
feelings started to change. It wasn't because of the sex. We
didn't have intercourse again for months, and when we did
it was disappointing. She was very shy at first. I think our
expectations of how good it would be once we knew each
other better, once we were having a genuine relationship,
were far too high.

I don't think kids are as desperate to have sex as the
media says. I think the television shows and the movies and
magazines create this so-called trend and some of the kids
think they have to do it to be like everyone else, whereas in
fact, everyone else isn't doing it at all.

Every girl I have ever had a relationship with has come
from a family with problems. Either the parents had split up
or they had been abused one way or another. None of these

girls was ever happy with me. They always ended up going off with someone who didn't treat them well – just like their parents or the adults in their lives had treated them.

That's why I don't like Joanna and why I don't want Helen having anything to do with her. It's a destructive need these girls have – to be with people who have been badly treated, to go back to people who will make sure they stay badly treated.

Joanna was always wanting Helen to go back to where they used to live, to see those blokes they used to hang out with. Once, after Rhett was born, I let Helen go. I drove her there and I left her with them. When I went to pick her up, she didn't want to come home with me. She wanted to stay with them. We had a bit of an argument but she finally got in the car. It was like Joanna had this magnet, pulling her back to where she thought she belonged.

All four of those kids came from the same sort of background – Joanna, Jeff, Matty and Helen. They are not unusual. That's the way most families in this area treat their kids. I'm the unusual one. My parents have been together for twenty-four years. They bicker but they don't bash each other. I had something to compare my own marriage to. I knew what it was supposed to be like. None of those kids do.

I went through a lot, talking Helen into keeping away from them. If she had decided to stay with Joanna that day, if she hadn't made the decision to come back to me, baby or no baby, I would not have married her. I knew I had to get her out of that self-destructive circle and if I couldn't do that, if she wouldn't do it, we would have no future.

Hopefully soon I will get a decent job and we can move out of here and live as a proper family in a place of our own.

The only thing I regret is that we missed out on what you would call a courtship. From the minute we started going out, we've been dealing with serious problems like finding a place to live and finding work and dealing with Helen's family difficulties and her pregnancy and then raising our own family on a low income. We've always had to be responsible and sensible.

It might have been fun to have had some time when we were just young and together.'

'I think I love you,' said Ben on the phone. It was so much easier on the phone. 'I'm sorry if I hurt your feelings at the beach, but I was confused. I've never been in love before.'

The camera was running again. The script was wonderful. Lucy held the receiver lovingly cupped against her ear. 'It's okay,' she whispered. 'I know. I'm confused too.'

'Come over,' said Ben. 'Come over to my house. There's nobody home. We could talk. Sort things out.'

'I'm going over to a friend's house, Dad,' she called. She was impressed with how normal she sounded, considering she felt all runny inside. Her dad was cooking dinner for one of his girlfriends. 'Where do we keep garlic salt?' he yelled. She put her head around the kitchen door. 'Top cupboard. And the number for takeaway pizza is on the fridge.' He threw a tea towel at her and she laughed and ducked and went to get her bike.

Ben was sitting on his front verandah. Lucy sat down beside him. They started talking quite normally, as if nothing had happened. Lucy didn't touch him or kiss him. Ben wished she would. He wondered what she expected him to do next. When both his older brothers came home unexpectedly early, he felt strangely relieved.

TEENAGE PARENTS: LEARNING TO LOVE, TRYING TO TRUST

Across the grassy park in front of the cluster of hospital buildings, a couple of kids were running, hand in hand. She was plump and rosy, a milkmaid dressed in a flapping turquoise tracksuit. He was thin, dark and all in brown, his thick hair tied back in a tangle of plaits. The girl shouted and waved as she bounded along, pulling him behind her.

On the verandah of the antenatal building, the small, thin woman in a rumpled nurse's uniform saw them, smiled and waved back.

'The baby is better and so am I,' panted the girl, flinging herself up against the wooden rail. 'We both had little infections and those antibiotic tablets have fixed us up.' She grinned. 'Isn't that great, Kaaren?'

'Me Mum's looking after the baby so Jill can have her checkup,' said the boy, 'but we came over to say thanks for helping us.'

They were both just fifteen years older than their brand new baby.

In Australia in 1996, more than eleven and a half thousand babies were born to young women aged between twelve and nineteen. The number of teenage pregnancies, which rose steeply in the 1970s, plateaued out again in the 1990s but pregnant teenagers continue to be of serious concern to those who have taken on the responsibility of helping them and their babies survive in a less than sympathetic world.

Our teenage birth rate is less than that of the United States and Britain, but compares poorly with European countries such as the Netherlands and Scandinavia, where sex education in schools is much more practical and explicit than it tends to be here.

Thankfully, the days when pregnant girls were cast out of their families and spurned by society as 'fallen women' are behind us. Most families support their daughters and adapt to the arrival of a new baby, even though this often means increased work and responsibility for the young women's mothers, whose child-rearing days were coming to an end. Gone too is the era when teenagers were persuaded to give up their babies for adoption; these days, to the chagrin of childless couples yearning to adopt children, adolescents who do not opt for a termination generally choose to keep their babies. Financial assistance from the government and a more tolerant (but not entirely approving) community make this possible.

In fact there is a popular theory among the middle classes that young women from disadvantaged backgrounds get pregnant on purpose in order to reap the financial awards. The good goss is that girls are just looking for guys to make them pregnant so they can get child support and stay away from work or school.

There's no doubt that a few young women, and their boyfriends too, cheat the system. However, it's much more likely that teenage pregnancy is high among girls from low socio-economic communities because they are the ones least likely to absorb the information they are given in health classes, or to use birth control, or to have the skills and the confidence to insist that their partners always use a condom.

There's another reason too. Some of the doctors and midwives who look after the girls when they become pregnant believe a large percentage of them are depressed.

Kaaren Dudley is a midwife who coordinates the adolescent pregnancy and parenting program at the Nepean Hospital in the Wentworth area, which nestles at the foot of the Blue Mountains in New South Wales. Here, in the far western suburbs of Sydney, the rate of teenage pregnancy is considerably higher than the state average. Kaaren has about seventy young women on her books each month and the numbers show no sign of diminishing.

Teenage pregnancy is a mental health issue, according to Kaaren, who believes that most of the young women in her care are clinically depressed.

'Up to 60% of these girls have been sexually abused at some time during their childhood or adolescence,' she said. 'They feel they have no control over their own bodies. For some of them, the only time they have been physically touched and loved is while they were being abused. They are sad. They want someone to love them so they offer sex, because that's all they know.

'They come here and tell their stories and some of them are really frightened of what we'll think of them, because they feel so ashamed. We get a lot of state wards who have never known what it's like to have a stable parent of their own. They say: "If I'd been a better girl my stepfather might not have beaten me." Or we get girls who have never had a mother to talk to, who say: "If I'd behaved when I was little Mum might have stayed around." We hear the same stories so many times.'

If the girls are less than twelve weeks pregnant when they come to the hospital, they are asked if they want to continue their pregnancies or to have them terminated. If they choose termination, an appointment is made with a social worker who will explain what this involves. The option of adoption is also explained to them.

'Most girls want to keep their babies,' said Kaaren. 'They have a need to love something. And often it gives them a reason for living.'

Antenatal (pre-pregnancy) care is very important for all pregnant women, but particularly so for those who have not previously been taught how to look after their health. 'You never tell them to give up anything,' said Kaaren. 'It only makes them do it twice as much. You just suggest cutting down. Smoke less than ten cigarettes a day. Cut back on the dope. Eat more fruit and vegetables. A lot of the girls are undernourished. We teach them about pap smears and breast checks and safe sex. The earlier they come to us, the more we can teach them about looking after themselves. If young people can't look after their own health, how can they properly care for their babies? They've never thought about it, mainly because they have never been properly parented themselves.'

Like most adolescent antenatal clinics, the team at Nepean Hospital encourages the young women to come along with their boyfriends. Research suggests that some young men remain involved for up to three years. They are almost always from a similar background to their partners.

There are always exceptions. One man turns up at Nepean regularly, always with a different girl. 'He's grown from a boy to a man since we've known him,' said Kaaren. 'He gets them pregnant and then he brings them in and hands them over to us.'

For middle-class families the situation is often different. 'The mothers ring me in a state of shock. We usually try to get the whole family to come in to our clinic to talk about it, so we can help them see that pregnancy is not the end of the world.'

Those who lose out in these cases can be the boys, who are often excluded from the pregnancy and birth by unforgiving families who close ranks against them. If their bond with the girl has been a close one, and they have accepted responsibility for fathering the child, this forced separation can mean a devastating sense of isolation which can result in severe and even life-threatening depression.

Young homeless girls are less likely to have family support, although their partners tend to hang around. The antenatal team arranges housing for couples who have nowhere to go.

The biggest hurdle for the hospital team is establishing trust. After years of regarding any government agency as their enemy, many young people are afraid their babies will be taken from them.

'We start off talking about their health and personal welfare and eventually we start talking about their feelings,' said Kaaren. 'Peer pressure and lack of self-esteem are the main reasons why most girls have sex. They have never dated as such. They don't "go out" as a couple. They don't deliberately become pregnant but they do have unprotected sex, often when they have been drinking or smoking dope.

'The young women often don't enjoy sex. I've had boys as well as girls talking to me about that and wondering why. Few of them know about foreplay or outercourse. It's just *wham bam thankyou ma'am* for most of them.

'We have to convince girls that they own their bodies. What happens to their bodies is up to them – even in the hospital. They have the right to say *no* to anyone.

'These kids have supposedly had sex education, but knowing what their different holes are for doesn't help them much. Sex education in schools doesn't work because it's not done in a practical way – and it's no fun. We show the boys how condoms can be put on in a way that gives sexual pleasure. We show them how to use lubricants to make it easier.

'Some of the girls have been given a prescription for the pill but that's the way it has stayed – words on a bit of paper. Some get it and take it for a few days. Some don't realise that if they vomit or get diarrhoea, it doesn't work.

'They all know about AIDS but hardly any of them know about the rest of the sexually transmitted diseases which they are far more likely to get. None of them know that hepatitis B can kill you.

'They want to know why they should be bothering with condoms when the girl is already pregnant. The deed is done. They don't think about the future.'

A majority of the girls who come to the clinics are aged between fourteen and seventeen. An exception was a 28-year-old woman who arrived at a hospital in labour – accompanied by her fourteen-year-old lover. 'He was wearing his school uniform,' recalled Kaaren. 'Neither of them seemed embarrassed.

'Some of the young women live in terror of their boyfriends. They come from domestic violence situations and they end up with men who treat them the same way as their fathers treated their mothers. They go back to trading sex for favours. "If I give him sex he'll let me have money to buy food instead of gambling it away." "If I give him sex he'll mind the baby so I can go out for a while."'

One girl came to the postnatal clinic and helped herself to about forty condoms. 'That should keep you going for a while,' said one of the nurses. 'For about a week,' the girl replied. 'If he doesn't get five fucks a day he bashes me. But if he does he gives me money to buy things for the baby.'

Just where the corridor widens in front of the lifts on the second floor, the adolescent antenatal team hunches on chairs at the weekly progress meeting. Their lack of facilities and limited numbers – there are four of them, managing about 250 teenage births each year – is reflected in similarly stretched operations in public hospitals throughout the country. The lift opens and a big, angry girl plods out and glares at the women on the half-circle of chairs.

'All right then, I'll do my own fucking examination,' she bellows. 'I haven't got all bloody day to sit around here.' As she strides away, her pregnant bulk protruding like a battering ram, a small woman scampering behind her turns and offers an apologetic smile to the antenatal team. This is her mother, who knows as well as they all do that the girl has all the time in the world.

'Of course some of the young women are difficult,' admitted Kaaren Dudley. 'Some of them don't care and count on their mothers doing everything. In a lot of cases, their mums have been down the same path and the girls are just continuing the pattern.'

A general practitioner who works with the antenatal team at Wentworth said the best way to help pregnant teenagers was to teach them how to help themselves. 'Many of them have never had any discipline so they find it hard to organise their lives,' she said. 'Some have never been taught the rules that the rest of us take for granted. They don't know about the little things – like not taking packets of chips into the consulting room when the doctor is examining them.'

Like speaking with respect to the people trying to help them?

'They expect people to help them,' said the GP. 'They are geared to a certain way of thinking – somehow somebody else will fix things. The system will always hand out the necessary money – not much, but enough to survive. Until they have their babies there is no incentive for them to do anything, and even then some of them rely on their mothers, who have to work so hard.

'These young people need help – but look at Mother Theresa. She helped millions of people but she did it by teaching them about responsibility.

'We've introduced a weekly craft session here where they can come along with their babies and learn basic living skills, like cooking and sewing. They love it.'

'Most teenage girls want to be good parents to their babies,' said Kaaren Dudley. 'They are willing to learn and they take their lessons seriously. Their babies are always beautifully dressed and spotlessly clean. If they do something wrong, and this is brought to their attention, these girls don't do it again.

'For many disadvantaged young women, having a baby turns their life around. They suddenly realise they have to think about the future. Some of them go back to school. Some enrol at TAFE colleges or university. Some settle down into a family situation with their boyfriends. Some of them get married. Most of them are terrific. They are brave and resilient and they try very hard. They are an inspiration to me.'

It was getting harder and harder for Ben and Lucy to find places where they could be alone together. His mother had finished with her meetings at the cliff house. Eventually he gave up indoor cricket. That meant he could be home on Saturday afternoons when everyone was out and Lucy usually came over.

They were doing less and less talking these days. It was all lips, hands, fingers, bodies, skin, soft moist flesh. They kissed and stroked and felt each other, touching places that they'd never touched before. 'Please,' Lucy would murmur as he kissed her and kissed her and reached into her jeans to rub his big hand over the curve of her smooth belly. 'Please, please...' He would gasp: 'What? What do you want me to do? Do you want me to...?' but she wouldn't say, she wouldn't discuss it, she just moaned softly, which made him so hard it hurt.

The thing was, it was making them both so cranky. They started arguing over stupid things. They were angry with each other, angry with their families, angry with themselves. He started getting jealous; she started saying bitchy, sarcastic things. Then they'd make up and start kissing and it was safer not to talk, it was better just to crawl into each other's arms and discover new and exciting things to do to one another.

She knew she had only to say 'yes' and the big thing would be done, it would be over, her virginity would be gone, lost, given to Ben. But if she said 'yes' the responsibility would be hers. And they would have to be all sensible and unromantic and worry about condoms and things. Whereas if it just happened, if it just happened the way it did on the screen, then nobody could be blamed, it would just be the magic of the moment. But then, if she got pregnant, it would be awful for everyone, not just her and Ben, but everyone. How would she ever tell her father? But how could she keep thinking sensibly when his sliding fingers were making her want to beg him to do it?

Finally, one horrible day, his mother came home unexpectedly early and found them feverishly entwining on the family-room couch. All she said was: 'Better put that boy down, Lucy, you don't know where he's been'. Lucy left in a sticky frenzy of humiliation. Ben was dishevelled, brick red and agonisingly embarrassed. He stomped into his room with Di in his disgusted wake.

'Don't say it Mum,' he said. 'I know what you're going to say, so don't bother.'

'I'll say what I like,' said Di. 'It's up to you whether you listen.'

She sat down on his bed, sighed, and looked out of the window. 'Oh no,' he thought. 'A major lecture.'

But his mother was brief. 'Love is a wonderful thing,' she said tersely. 'Sex, on the other hand, can be very dangerous in the hands of the young and inexperienced.'

'Not that it's any of your business,' said Ben, 'but we're not having sex.'

His mother gave him her steady, level look. He finally forced himself to look back.

'You may not be having sexual intercourse with Lucy,' she said. 'But from what I just saw, you are both having a fair bit of sex. Be very careful, Ben. I'm too young to be a grandmother. You're not too young to catch a disease. If you must do it, and I sincerely hope you won't, I hope you know how to use a condom.'

'I said we're not having sex. We just love each other, that's all. What's so horribly wrong with that?'

Di sighed and got up. 'Nothing's wrong with love, Ben. You know that as well as I do. Just make sure you both think about the difference between love and sex. It's easy to get them confused.'

She went to the door and glanced back at him. 'I hope Lucy realises that her shirt is on inside out before she gets home.'

HOMOSEXUALITY: TO BE OR NOT TO BE - THAT IS THE QUESTION

At some stage during their adolescence, almost all teenagers will question the direction of their sexuality. Boys will wonder if they are attracted to other boys; girls to other girls. Some young people realise from an early age that they are homosexual; others wrestle with the issue for many troubled years.

Homosexuals are people who prefer to have sexual relationships with people of the same sex as them. The modern and somewhat misleading term for homosexual men and women is 'gay', which is not a particularly accurate term because for many people, and particularly young people, their homosexuality is a confusing and serious problem. Homosexual women are commonly called lesbians.

Bisexual people enjoy having sex with members of either sex.

A national study of attitudes to sexuality carried out by La Trobe University in Victoria in 1997 revealed that 8% of Year Ten students and 9% of Year Twelve students had experienced feelings that were not exclusively heterosexual. Only 3% of the students surveyed said they were attracted exclusively to people of the same sex.

Same sex relations between men involve kissing, hugging, mutual masturbation, oral sex and anal sex. Women make love to each other by kissing, hugging, mutual masturbation, oral sex and penetration of the vagina and anus with fingers, hands and, sometimes, sex aids.

Until very recently our society has had little tolerance of homosexuality, believing it to be a perverted lifestyle choice rather than a natural phenomenon over which the people concerned have no control. This situation is now gradually changing, mainly as a result of the increasingly public profile that gay and lesbian organisations have attained over the past thirty years in Australia.

WHAT IF YOU ARE ...

Research now suggests that a person's sexual orientation is determined early in life and cannot be changed or 'cured'. Gay adolescents generally feel different for a long time and struggle alone with uncertainty, confusion and fear. Uncertain, angry and desperately worried about themselves and their future, they usually develop very low self-esteem and are much more likely than their peers to suffer from depression and to attempt or commit suicide. They often take out their rage and frustration in dangerous and destructive behaviour, blotting out reality with binge drinking or drugs.

There are also homosexual young people in our community who do nothing at all to attract attention to themselves, but who suffer from the unbearable loneliness of those who simply do not belong.

Although some confide in their friends, most young gay people are too terrified to tell their parents the way they feel. In his book *Growing Pains*, David Bennett writes: 'When the subject of a young person's homosexuality is ultimately broached with parents, there is no way for it not to be a shock. As this is unlikely to be what they wanted for their child, there is a grieving process to go through, involving denial, guilt, self-doubt and anger. "What will family and friends think when they find out? Am I to blame in some way? Could it have been prevented?" Or more selfishly, "Why are you doing this to us?" Getting used to the idea takes time and it is often helpful in this situation to talk with other parents of gay youths. The support and advice that can be provided by a group is usually worth enlisting.

'On the other hand, many parents take great pride in their gay and lesbian children and express hostility towards the unfair societal victimisation they often suffer.'

As with every other aspect of sex education, the main thing parents and their gay children need to do is to talk to each other about it. Even if it hurts like hell at first, communication within families can save heartbreak, mental illness and alienation further down the track.

Although a more tolerant attitude to homosexuality is developing in most western communities, the acceptance of gay men has been severely set back by the spread of the highly contagious HIV virus (which can lead to AIDS). For young gay and bisexual males, unprotected anal intercourse puts them at extreme risk of contracting sexually trans-mitted diseases like HIV and hepatitis B.

There is nothing wrong or shameful about being gay, although it means you are part of a minority group. There is nothing wrong or shameful about not being gay, although it means you will always be one of the majority. There is a great deal wrong about being anti-gay and people who claim to despise and dislike gays and lesbians may be hiding hang-ups of their own. Fortunately, while homophobic (gay-hating) people used to be in the majority in Australia, they too are becoming a minority group. It is up to young people (and, hopefully, their parents) to trample on the prejudice of previous generations and accept that while a small percentage of their peers have a different sexual preference to the majority, in almost every other way they are just like everybody else.

...BUT WHAT IF YOU'RE NOT?

Having a crush on a friend of the same sex, or even on an older person, is a perfectly normal part of childhood and adolescence. However, quite a lot of young people go further. In the process of trying to understand their sexuality, some of them have sexual experiences with people of the same sex.

Whether or not they enjoy the adventure, this does not make them homosexuals, just as eating vegetables and nuts for a week wouldn't make them vegetarians. It does worry them a lot more than a fruit-and-nut diet, however, and can cause terrible distress and even tragic consequences as they convince themselves most unhappily that they must be gay. Their struggle to find answers to whether or not they are really 'different' can be a long, lonely and disillusioning one.

Young people can't help but be influenced by the media, which is fascinated by almost anything to do with the homosexual community and attracts many gay people to its creative ranks. Sydney's Gay and Lesbian Mardi Gras has become an international tourist attraction, with all the attendant publicity that involves. Inevitably, teenagers who might never have thought about being gay a generation ago now torture themselves with doubt.

Their problems can get even more complicated when they receive sympathy and support from the gay community and considerably less understanding from heterosexual friends and family. Their sexual confusion is a particularly difficult problem to discuss, but discussion and reassurance from an older and wiser person is what they desperately need.

So if you are a parent with an adolescent who might be in this predicament, don't panic. Bring it up. Talk about it. Be there. Listen. Try to understand.

Like many adolescent problems, this may be a phase that will pass. If it doesn't, the fact that you are already talking will make it easier for you both.

GOOD READING

Homosexuality does not simply come down to boys having sex with boys, and girls with girls. As well as physical homosexuality, a person's culture, emotional attachments and private fantasies mean that being gay (or not being gay, but being strongly attracted to members of the same sex) is never straightforward.

Homosexuality is a very difficult and complex issue which cannot be thoroughly covered in this book. Fortunately, many excellent books have been written to help both parents and their homosexual adolescents demolish the myths and prejudices and come to terms with the realities of being gay. A list is provided on page 251.

TRANSGENDER ADOLESCENTS

A small number of young people spend their entire childhood wondering whether there was a bit of a muddle-up when Father God or Mother Nature was handing out the gender hormones. The boys want to be girls. The girls want to be boys. Often these (generally suppressed) yearnings reach their peak during adolescence.

Transgender people are not necessarily homosexual. Some are happily married.

Not surprisingly, it is almost impossible for parents to face a problem like this one. Nevertheless, it is very important not to over-react in this situation and, once again, to talk to the young person concerned. Finding out what's going on in their mind and heart is the beginning of the way through. Without doubt, this will be an extraordinarily difficult thing to face and to do – but do try.

Specialist counselling for parents and kids is available for transgender issues. Start with community health centres.

GERRY'S STORY

'I'll wait outside the station,' she said. 'I'll be the big hairy one, of course.' In fact she is not tall and her hair is very short – dark, crisp curls held in place with mousse. She has never worn makeup and her face is rosy, with a few spots. She wears glasses with light, elegant frames, and her eyes, brown and frank, are clearly visible beneath clearly defined brows. It's hard to tell what sort of body she has, as it is swamped in a sloppy jumper, but she is neither fat nor thin. The only aspect of her appearance that might make her stand out in a crowd is her purple shoes with their green and black laces – but even then it would depend on the crowd in question.

Gerry has never been one of the crowd. She has always been bright, but at school she never quite made it into the cool groups. She was handicapped by shyness and a sometimes overwhelming feeling of isolation. Since leaving school she has become more confident; she has learned some impressive university-speak, although most of her sentences still conclude with the upward tilt that's a leftover from her suburban childhood.

At nineteen, Gerry still lives with her parents in an ordinary house in an ordinary street and her parents are nice, ordinary, normal folk. Her mother is a housewife. Her father sells life insurance. Her brother is much older and left home long ago. He has always been in trouble but she has always been a good girl. For reasons she can't fathom, he's still the favourite.

Gerry spends several nights a week at the city terrace house of her friend Sophie. It's closer to the university where she is studying arts. And there are other advantages.

'The first thing I can remember about my sexual feelings is feeling terribly left out in Year Five and Year Six, when kids start thinking about "going out" and kissing and stuff like that. I only had one close friend in primary school. I got on better with adults – I was quite intelligent, which might have something to do with it. I was terribly shy and I had a crush on this boy called Malcolm who lived next door. I asked him if he was my best friend and he said he was, but I told him he couldn't be mine because nobody could love their best friend the way I loved him.

My mother sent me to a "where does your baby come from" night at the school and I remember thinking that I already knew all about that, from hearing people talk and from television. My parents never talked to me about sex, not ever. They are very uncomfortable about that sort of thing. You can feel the tension in the house whenever something sexual comes on the television. Nobody will look at each other. When I got my periods in Year Six my mother told me what it was, but I already knew.

When I developed breasts and when other signs of puberty came, I was very embarrassed. I refused to wear a bra unless it was absolutely necessary. I couldn't bear the thought of being humiliated by the boys who snapped girls' bra straps.

I was very anxious about starting high school, mainly because I didn't know anybody. I had a boyfriend for a couple of days in Year Seven but I got sick of him and pushed him over one day and I kicked him as well. I can't remember why. He was a little creep and still is – he has probably been pushed over by many a girl since.

I had another boyfriend on and off during Year Eight and Year Nine. Phil was skinny and shorter than me, although eventually he grew. He wasn't popular and neither was I, which might have been part of the appeal. I knew he wouldn't be able to humiliate me the way other boys did. It was the usual adolescent fumbling thing – I wrote him a letter telling him he could touch my breasts. We communicated best through writing letters to each other. When we were actually together we didn't have much to say to each other. Kissing him wasn't all that enjoyable, but it gave me status. I was intensely uncomfortable when he unbuttoned my shirt and looked at my breasts. I hate my breasts. One is a different shape and size to the other. I've recently found out that this is not at all unusual but I didn't know it then and it was a serious worry for me.

We fought a lot because he was very jealous of another boy, a friend I had made named Mark, who was an incredibly good dancer and very graceful. He spoke with a bit of a lisp and he got teased a lot at school. We got on very well. I couldn't define the difference between the way I felt about these two boys, but although the difference was very obvious to me, it wasn't at all obvious to Phil.

For a couple of weeks after I broke up with Phil I went out with Mark. We used to kiss but it just didn't feel right. So I said to him: "This isn't working, is it?" and he said: "No, it's not. Let's just be friends." We've been friends ever since.

At the beginning of Year Ten I was doing an acting workshop at weekends. Most of the other students were older and, being drama students, the girls were grungy and bizarre looking. This really appealed to me. One night I had a sexual dream about one of these girls, whose name was Skye. I started to wonder if I was a lesbian. I was quite depressed. There was a gay teacher at our school and I talked to him and to Mark, but they both said dreaming about girls didn't mean I was a lesbian — that it was quite normal for adolescents to get crushes on people of the same sex.

I never thought to myself: "Oh my God, what if I *am* one?" I didn't care a bit if I was a lesbian or not. But I was very worried about how I would ever find out. I had no confidence in myself. I didn't know anyone to talk to. Mark was wondering about himself at the same time, but it was a case of the blind leading the blind.

Skye was quite different looking to the rest of us. She dyed her hair and wore weird clothes and was into art and music. She frightened me.

By this time I did have some friends and they were all wondering why I was so depressed. Eventually I told them I thought I might be a lesbian and they were very supportive. One of them spoke to Skye for me and she invited me to come and talk to her.

We stood together on a piece of scaffolding while she was painting a backdrop and she told me she was bisexual and she knew what I was going through. She became my idol, the rock that I clung to while I was overwhelmed with worry. I remember asking her if I could kiss her, because I still didn't know how it would feel to have physical contact with a woman. Skye said it would be better if I found someone and discovered those feelings for myself. At the time I was devastated but now I'm glad because when I finally had my first kiss it was something quite amazing.

One day shortly after that, I decided I didn't need to kiss anyone to find out because I just knew. I just thought: "I am a lesbian." It was a relief in a way. I told Skye and she was very happy for me. One by one I told my close friends.

Eventually everyone in my grade knew and I started to feel that my parents had the right to know too. But I was afraid to tell them. I don't know why. It's not as if they have ever hit me or treated me badly. There has never been any emotional blackmail or anything like that. We talk – we discuss political events and what is going on in the world and what I am studying. But they never ask what is going on in my life. I know there are rules about that, but I don't know what the rules are.

I never think my parents are right about anything to do with me. There is a definite lack of emotional honesty in their relationship with me. But despite that, I am still afraid of losing them. For some reason I don't understand, I really care about what they think about me and I always want their approval.

Mark came out as a gay shortly after me, so we supported each other. He was hassled a lot more than I was at school. He couldn't go into the playground without being called a faggot. I was never teased at school – far from it. I had never been one of the cool crowd, but in the senior years of high school I started mixing with a lot of other students, including the popular ones. Because I was a lesbian they were always asking me things. I answered their questions till I was blue in the face.

I had my first kiss from a girl who came to my sixteenth birthday party. After the others left we were in my room, playing with each other's hair and stuff and talking about her problems. It was just – like – electric! I pointed out to her that we were just dancing around our feelings and she said: "Look, I just don't want to hurt you." So I said: "Why not let me make that decision for myself?" We kissed then, just once. I felt it all through my body. I could still feel it days afterwards. I was very excited. For me it was the final confirmation that I needed.

It meant very little to that particular girl, who was older than me and had just left our school. We didn't have much more to do with each other after that night, although I had a stupid crush on her for a while. I get stupid crushes on people.

Since then I have lived with the continual awareness that I am a lesbian. It's always there. At first I felt very alone. I was depressed because I was different and I thought nobody understood me.

I wasn't really in a position to find groups who could help me, or to get counselling or anything like that because I was only allowed to go out if my parents knew where I was going and I would have had to lie to them. I wasn't game to ring any places in case the phone number appeared on my parents' bill.

I was in Year Eleven and feeling very depressed at the prospect of being misunderstood and very much alone for the rest of my life when I met a younger girl, called Sharon, who was bisexual and needed to talk about her problems. We decided to get together, even though I felt a bit bad about her being only fourteen. But she needed the sort of support I would have liked when I was her age.

Her mother was bisexual and her family was very open. They knew we were together. When I went in their car once, her younger brother sat in the front and said: 'I'm leaving the back seat for you two!' I was so uncomfortable with all that – it wasn't what I used to.

Kissing Sharon wasn't as wonderful as that first time, but you wouldn't expect it to be. One day at her place we were kissing and we took our clothes off and touched each other's bodies. She decided to get yoghurt and put it all over the front of me so she could lick it off. That was quite funny. When we started having sex I knew what to do. I suppose it's because both our anatomies were the same, but I knew what would give her pleasure. I'm not sure whether I put my fingers inside her first or whether I licked her out first but eventually I did both things and she licked me out too. I just stopped when I thought we'd had enough but I think she came – it's just that back then I wouldn't have known what that was.

Afterwards I felt I had made a mistake and even though it was fully consensual I had problems with her age. She was very intelligent and very mature but I felt ashamed and my bad feelings spoiled what might have been a very good experience. I broke it off eventually because of my own guilt and because I couldn't deal with the way her family was so approving of it all. Several months later I wrote to her and apologised for the way I had treated her and she was cool about it.

Later in that year I met the daughter of a business associate of my father's. When you're homosexual you develop a bit of a radar. Something triggered when I met Alana. I came out to her one day and she told me she was a lesbian too and it was like, both of us going "yay!" She was my first lesbian friend. We kissed a lot but we never had sex. She hated being a lesbian. She decided to get a boyfriend and pretend to be straight. She was very self-destructive. I tried to be there for her but she had too many problems.

Because our fathers knew each other I thought the time had come to tell my parents before someone else did. I was terribly worried about it. My family life isn't bad – just short on love, I think. My brother has been getting into trouble all his life, with the police and drugs and everything – basically he has never been the ideal child, but I have. I'm at uni and I've never been in trouble, I've never used drugs and I'm trying to do something with my life and I am very responsible. But he is still the favourite. They bail him out every time he makes a bad decision. It hurts me a lot that my mother seems to love him more than she loves me.

I decided to break the news one weekend and I wrote a letter in case I was too emotional to explain myself to them and I packed a bag, just in case, as I wasn't sure what their reaction would be. It was such an intensely painful period that I can't remember a lot about it. I put it off until the end of the weekend and on the Sunday afternoon I said to them: "I need to tell you something." I told them I was a lesbian. My mum cried. She said: "I knew this was coming but now it's here I don't know what to say." My dad said: "You know we love you anyway, and it doesn't matter to us who you are or what you are – but if you change your mind, that's okay as well."

Some of my lesbian friends have suggested that maybe my dad is gay – maybe that's why he was more accepting than Mum.'

It is difficult for her to discuss her parents. She can't explain what's wrong with them or why she wants their love, but not their approval. She closes her eyes disdainfully at the suggestion that her attitude to them has put her parents firmly in a lose–lose situation.

'I doubt that my mum has told anyone ever that I am a lesbian. It comes as a shock to her that other people know. I know my dad has told some people. Anyway, everyone comes up with theories about their attitude.

I was never discriminated against at school but I always had the feeling the others just wished I wasn't there. In Year Twelve, Mark and I went to our teachers and complained about the homophobic jokes and the harassment that Mark was getting every day. As a result, the principal implemented a day of workshops and panel discussions on homophobia and gender issues. That day made a difference to me; the people who came to our school to run it were the first gay and lesbian people I had met, apart from Mark and my teacher.

I also had a very accepting and loving drama teacher who helped me a lot, who taught me that even though it is natural to think seriously about a lot of the things that happen in life, it is still okay to be happy. I tend to be a depressed sort of person – I have to make a real effort to be happy.

I studied very hard for my final exams and I got very high marks. When school finished, Mark and I went to Melbourne for a holiday and we visited a gay and lesbian club. He picked up a guy and went off to dance. I was left by myself and I didn't know what to do and I felt completely inadequate. I had been thinking that as soon as I got into the gay and lesbian scene I wouldn't feel so alone, but there I was, and I felt worse! I didn't know the rules. I was really depressed.

This bizarre guy in a top hat, no shirt, a bow tie and pants sat down and talked to me but I couldn't understand what he was saying. Then he brought over this young girl and she started kissing me. I really didn't know how to stop it. She took me into a cubicle in the toilets and started making out with me and asking if she could take me home and fuck me and all this stuff. She was only about seventeen and she was very drunk. I was absolutely terrified. I said no, I didn't want to go home with her and couldn't we just keep doing what we were doing? Finally I got out of the cubicle and she picked up an empty bottle and smashed it and I didn't know if she was going to attack me or herself. I raced out and told her friend in the hat to go and help her and that was that. It was a most unpleasant experience.

I didn't stop feeling alone until I started university, where people are much more accepting of everyone. I didn't join any lesbian groups the first year because I couldn't find the room they met in, but I've joined them this year. At first I was a bit scared of lesbians. I didn't know how to interact with them. I didn't know the rules.

At uni I was very worried about the work load and coping with the long hours of commuting between home and the city. I was lonely until I met Ed, who is gay and who has become a very close friend. He is twenty-three and very interesting and experienced in every way.

I met my next girlfriend, Kathy, halfway through my first year. She was pretty, with short red hair, very sophisticated, but dumpy. I would never have guessed she was a lesbian. We started meeting for coffee and talking and I fell in love with her very quickly. I wanted to experiment with sex and as she had her own flat we tried a lot of things together. I stayed at her house two or three nights a week and we had sex a lot, two or three times a night I suppose, although with lesbian sex it's hard to say where it begins and ends.

Sex with girls is always basically the same. You enter each other with fingers and hands or you have oral sex with tongues. We never used sex toys or did anything kinky. We tried some different positions.

Physically it's very hard for me to enjoy sex. I have to be very turned on for it to be a pleasure. I never have an orgasm. But I am a very competitive person and I like to be good at what I do. I was a bit embarrassed at not being able to do things well.

We had sex in toilet cubicles and we were a bit naughty with each other in public, which I enjoyed. It's a bit of a political statement for me. I refuse to monitor my behaviour according to other people's prejudices so if I feel like kissing my girlfriend in public, that's what I will do. That resulted in us getting abused a few times. Some lunatic at a train station once threatened to break our kneecaps because we were filthy. On another station a bloke said we were the reason he couldn't get a girlfriend. Like sure! That's exactly why we became lesbians, just to stop him getting a woman!

Like all my girlfriends, Kathy had a lot of problems, although she wouldn't share many of them with me. There was an underlying darkness to her. I know she loved me but I think she loved me too much and she didn't know what to do with that love. We started fighting. We never communicated properly. After three months she broke it off and I couldn't get in touch with her for days – I left a lecture balling my eyes out because I didn't know what was going on.

The next morning, as soon as Mum saw me she knew something was wrong. When she said "How are you?"

I broke down. She sort of patted me on the head and I told her I was going to force a confrontation with Kathy that day but Mum said Kathy might not be able to give me any answers. "Just try and maintain some dignity," was my mother's typical advice.

I wore my ripped jeans because I knew they were Kathy's favourites. I made a complete idiot of myself, sobbing and crying and shuddering – all of that. I was in the sort of pain that I hope never to experience again. She couldn't handle it and she couldn't give me any answers.

Ed was waiting for me with Dana, another good friend from uni. I cried for about half an hour without stopping. When I finally stopped, I said to them both: "Dignity was *not* maintained." I was exhausted after that. I didn't care if I lived or died.

A few days later I was at a party at Dana's house and we were both drunk on cheap bourbon – I don't do drugs but I've been drinking more since I left school – and she suddenly started touching me and stuff. I thought she was straight, but we ended up in a drunken mess, with our pants down, having sex on her father's bed. I sobered up pretty quickly when someone came in and asked her where they might find a screwdriver – and then nicely turned out the light for us as they left. Dana threw up afterwards.

We spent the night in bed together and she told me she had been attracted to me since we had first met. We decided we were fuck buddies – we would have sex with each other as friends but nothing more. Of course, it's never as uncomplicated as that and I ended up falling in love with her. Having sex with her became addictive – I knew it was bad for me but I wasn't ready to stop. One night Ed and Dana and I ended up at her place and we had sex as a threesome – none of it was penetrative but it was good for him to have a loving experience with his two favourite women. We never did it again and it has become a bit of a joke between us.

I met Sophie three months ago. She is an American student on exchange from the States and she is a couple of years older than me. I met her at a Queer Girls party at uni and then we went to a nightclub and danced. I took off my shirt and danced quite dirtily and we kissed for about an hour but we didn't see each other again for a couple of weeks. We met up again at a club and I was actually after another girl but we danced for a while and eventually we went to her place. She told me she had another girlfriend in America and we were just going to share her bed but she couldn't keep her hands off me. We've been a couple ever since.

Sophie is tall and very fit and athletic. She likes working out at the gym. She has red hair and hazel eyes which change colour and she is a very womanly shape. She is very practical. She loves dressing up and wearing little skirts and tiny tops. I don't. I feel more comfortable in pants.

Our relationship started off as purely sexual but since then it has become very emotional as well – we have candle-lit dinners and we talk a lot. It's very romantic. The sex has evolved into something different. We've experimented more than ever before. She likes to use a vibrator and she likes being tied up. I like it too, but not my legs. It's different and it turns me on. We had a disaster recently with some chocolate topping – we used too much and it made me sick and it went hard too quickly. We laugh a lot, which is something I've never done before with any of my lovers.

We're still getting to know each other but I am thinking of going back to America with her next year.

My mother has a lot of trouble with my sexuality. If anything is not what she thinks is normal, she prefers it to go away. But Sophie has been very good for my family. She comes to family things with me and she is very friendly and they really like her. She is very intelligent and very feminine. Our household has been much happier since I've been with Sophie, which is very ironic.

I didn't choose to be a lesbian. I did choose not to hide it. I'm not sure if I was born like this or if it was socially constructed in me, but this is how I am and I doubt if I will ever change. I think when people say they were born with it, it's an excuse. It's like saying it isn't their fault. I also think it's very dangerous to look for a "gay gene" because that could lead to the abortion of gay and lesbian foetuses. This would "fix" what people see as a problem, rather than a viable alternative to sexuality.

It's not necessary to ask how or why I became this way. Nobody asks straight people how or why they became the way they are.

There is still a lot of ignorance about sexuality and many people are very misunderstood. But it doesn't take very much to plant the idea in people's minds that there is nothing wrong with people who are homosexual – and that it is a natural state for them.

I've always had trouble with the concept of marriage. You don't need to make a commitment to someone while you're wearing a big white dress and standing in front of 150 people to make it real. Sophie wants to get married one day though, because she wants the big white dress. It's not yet legal for same sex people to get married but there are such things as commitment ceremonies. And the law is changing for same sex couples in other areas.

I never wanted to have children, but this year I have really started wanting a child. Ed and I talk about it a lot – having a child together and raising it together as the ultimate act of friendship. Sophie and I have talked about it too – how we would raise a child. So it's a definite possibility for us.

I am not a religious person in any way. Sophie is. But I would never cheat the person I loved and I would expect to trust her as well. What I want most of all out of life is monogamy and a family of my own.'

Lucy crept up the stairs and into her room. She turned on the shower full blast and tried to wash away her embarrassment and mortification, not to mention a lot of Ben's saliva and some other sticky fluids she didn't want to think about. It didn't work. When she got out of the shower she felt even worse. She kept seeing that awful picture in her mind, the two of them half-dressed, pawing each other and heaving and panting like animals and Ben's mother, always so neat and clean, coming in and seeing them like that, hearing them like that. It was so...so...undignified. So downright horrible.

She dried herself, put on her ancient and shabby dressing gown and sat on the bed. She stared at her reflection in the mirror hanging on her cupboard door. She was never very sure about the way she looked. Her face always seemed to need colouring in. She wished she knew someone older and wiser who could teach her how to put makeup on. Now her hair hung down rattily around her cheeks. Her face and eyes were puffy. Her neck and chest were covered in red blotches. She felt ugly. She felt dirty. She started to cry.

For the first time in ages she wished her mother was around.

She didn't know how long her father had been standing in the doorway. When he sat down beside her on the bed she nearly jumped out of her skin for the second time that day.

'What's up kid o' mine?' he asked in his rumbly brown voice. 'Trouble at mill?'

She cried as if she would never stop and her dad put his skinny, hairy arms around her and rubbed her back and made soothing noises and said 'Shhh' now and then, the way he'd done since she was a baby. Then he got up and brought over a box of tissues from her dressing table and offered her three so she could blow her nose. It was a thing he always did – three tissues at a time. Not two, never one. Always three. The thought made her smile, for some silly reason.

'That's better,' he said. 'Boy trouble is it then? You and your young bloke have a row?'

'No,' she said. 'We were...having a bit of a cuddle...and his mother came in...and ...' She stopped. It was too awful to think about, let alone explain.

'Aah,' said her dad thoughtfully. He looked at her in the mirror and she lowered her eyes and wouldn't look back. 'Aah,' he said again. Then he gave her a little squeeze and got up. 'I'd better let you get dressed,' he said. 'I think what we both need is a cup of tea.'

When she went into the kitchen he put two steaming cups on the chipped wooden table and they sat opposite each other on wobbly chairs and sipped their tea slowly. Lucy couldn't think of anything to say. All she wanted to do was blot out the events of the afternoon.

Finally her dad said: 'I suppose you thought I wouldn't mind.'

Lucy was startled out of her thoughts. She blinked at him. 'Wouldn't mind what?'

He sighed. 'Wouldn't mind you fooling around with your young bloke. I suppose you thought what's good for the gander is good for the goose.'

'I don't know what you're talking about, Dad,' said Lucy.

He sighed again. 'I haven't set you a very good example, have I love? All these lovely lady friends of mine. They're hard to resist but I don't even try, do I?'

Lucy shrugged. 'You're on your own. You probably need to cheer yourself up.'

Her dad looked at his hands. Then he cleared his throat.

'Listen to me, love,' he said slowly. 'I'm not on my own. I have Gregory and I have you.' He reached out and took her teacup away from her. Then he held both her hands tightly in his.

'You are more important to me than anyone. You always have been. You always will be. You're my lovely daughter, you're a treasure. You're even gorgeous to look at.'

'You're lovely,' he repeated, when she shook her head. 'And what you have to offer some very lucky bloke is very very special. It's more than special. It's precious, like you.' He paused and squeezed her hands tightly. 'Don't give it away too soon.'

CONTRACEPTION: PREVENTION IS BETTER THAN PAIN

There are two reasons for using contraception during sexual intercourse:
- To prevent a girl from becoming pregnant;
- To prevent a girl and a boy from getting a sexually transmissible disease.

The only contraceptive device that does both is the condom.

CONDOMS

A condom is a fine rubber cover which must be fitted onto an erect penis just before intercourse. When the wearer ejaculates, the sperm remains inside the condom instead of entering the vagina and uterus.

The condom is enjoying a huge increase in popularity, probably because it's cheap and easy to use, feels good, tastes okay and can do two things at the same time. Once the condom was an embarrassment to itself and others. It was called a french letter, a rubber, a sheath or a sleeve. These days people tend to call it by its real name because it's no longer pretending to be something else.

The condom has a practical, sensible function. By keeping kids safe from disease, it is making a genuinely useful contribution to the community. It is also keeping unborn babies out of the world until people are actually ready to have them.

These days sex educators are wild about the condom, parents with common sense are happy knowing it's easily available and even the crankiest school teachers admit grudgingly that if kids insist on having sex, the ones who do it with a condom on have more brains than their school reports suggest.

Girls like condoms because using them means boys have to take some of the responsibility for contraception. On the other hand, just in case the boys don't have any, sensible young women always keep a supply of their own handy if they have decided to have sex.

The condom is available from family planning and health clinics, pharmacies, supermarkets and vending machines. An ordinary one costs about sixty cents, although they usually come in packets of four or more. Condoms also come in different styles, colours and flavours.

Condoms work well if they are used properly. This means using a new one every time sex takes place, and being careful to put it on and take it off correctly, so that none of the sperm spills out. A water-based lubricant such as KY Jelly or Wet Stuff should be used every time a condom is worn, to reduce the risk of it breaking. This lubricant is rubbed over the condom when it's on, which can be a rather enjoyable feeling, especially if the other person is doing it. In fact, using a condom can be heaps of fun.

PUTTING ON A CONDOM

1. If you've never used a condom before, practise first.
2. Check the use-by date on the packet. Rubber is perishable and can break. When you remove the condom, don't snag it with rings or fingernails.

3. Put the condom on before sexual contact. Roll it on, holding an extra bit at the tip to allow room for the semen.
4. Roll it all the way to the base of the penis.
5. Rub lubricant over the condom.
6. When withdrawing the penis from the vagina (or anus), hold on to the rim or edge of the condom.
7. Pull the condom off carefully, making sure none of the semen inside spills into the vaginal or anal area.
8. Wrap the used condom in scrap paper and put it in the garbage bin, not down the toilet.

If you've very sensibly bought some condoms, but then even more sensibly decided against sexual intercourse until you're older, condoms make great water bombs.

THE PILL

Depending on your point of view, your religion, your moral beliefs and your age, the pill is either a blessing or a curse. It has made birth control simple and easy. But by removing the fear of pregnancy it has created sexual freedom and some people believe it has brought about the moral deterioration of our society. Women have benefited enormously from the pill, although it has put the responsibility for contraception firmly in the female court. In fact, the increasing popularity of the condom evens things up quite nicely as the most effective way to avoid both pregnancy and STDs is to use both.

There are two main types of oral contraceptive pill. Both must be taken daily. The combined pill contains two hormones, oestrogen and progestogen, which stop the ovaries releasing an egg each month. It is 99% effective. The minipill, which is slightly less effective and must be taken at exactly the same time each day, uses progestogen only and works by changing the mucus at the entrance to the womb (uterus) so that sperm cannot pass through to fertilise the egg. Both pills must be taken for seven days and preferably a month, before they start working properly.

The pill is easy to use as it has only to be taken once a day, with nothing extra involved when having sex. It can be prescribed by a health clinic or general practitioner. The pill makes periods come regularly and can improve acne and PMT. However, some people gain weight, or suffer headaches, sore breasts and slight bleeding (spotting) between periods. Sometimes a young woman needs to try different brands of pill to find one that agrees with her. Smoking increases the health risks of taking the pill.

DIAPHRAGMS AND CERVICAL CAPS

A diaphragm is a soft rubber cap worn inside the vagina. It covers the cervix, which is the entrance to the uterus. It prevents the male's sperm from entering the uterus.

Diaphragms must be inserted just before having sex. If they fit properly and have been properly put in and are used every time a couple has intercourse, they work well. They don't interfere with any body functions. A diaphragm must be bought from a pharmacy or clinic and fitted by a nurse or doctor, who will also teach the young woman how to insert it properly.

THE IUD

The intrauterine device or IUD is a small plastic or plastic and copper object which a doctor puts inside a woman's uterus (womb). It prevents the fertilised egg from planting itself in the uterus to begin a pregnancy. It is 98% effective. Side effects can involve heavier and longer periods and cramps. An IUD can stay in for four years or even longer. It is not recommended for girls using contraception for the first time.

DEPO PROVERA

This is a synthetic hormone which is given by injection every three months. It is 99% effective in preventing conception. Side-effects involve changes in period bleeding. It must be administered by a qualified medical practitioner.

THE MORNING-AFTER PILL

For a young woman who had sex when she didn't plan to, or whose partner used a condom which broke, the morning-after pill is available from Family Planning clinics and some GPs. There are actually four pills which must be taken no more than three days after unprotected sex. It is essential to take two of the pills as soon as possible and two more exactly twelve hours later.

The morning-after pill stops a woman's ovary making an egg. If the egg has already been made it stops the fertilised egg from implanting in the womb. About half the women who use it feel sick during treatment, although anti-nausea tablets are usually prescribed along with the pill.

OTHER METHODS

There are three other methods of birth control that people can use. However, they are not reliable unless used along with one of the more effective contraceptives described above.

SPERMICIDES

These are creams, foams, gels or vaginal tablets which are put in the vagina before sex. They are available from clinics or pharmacies.

THE RHYTHM METHOD

This is also called the Billings, mucus, ovulation or temperature method. It involves avoiding sex during those times of a woman's monthly cycle when she is most likely to become pregnant. It takes a lot of practice, enormous will-power and a very thorough knowledge of her own body.

WITHDRAWAL

A man can attempt to prevent making a woman pregnant by withdrawing his penis from her vagina before ejaculation. It takes a huge amount of willpower for a man, particularly a young inexperienced man, to do this. If he doesn't manage it, if he forgets or if he isn't quick enough, it doesn't work. Also, there may be some sperm in the fluid that comes out of his penis before he 'comes'. Even if he ejaculates at the entrance to the vagina, some sperm can swim inside. In their quest to make new life against all odds, these little guys are quite determined.

So if the boy tells the girl he's only going to put it in for a minute or two, she shouldn't be persuaded. She'd be a lot safer providing him with a condom or, better still, telling him she's not a microwave and sending him home.

REMEMBER, WHEN IT COMES TO CONTRACEPTION:

- Don't be silly, protect your willy!
- You can't go wrong if you shield your dong!
- It will be sweeter if you wrap your tweeter!
- CONDOMS RULE!

JULIA'S STORY

Hannah was right. Her friend Julia, who 'gets boys really easily', is gorgeous. She has enormous eyes and a mass of thick, curly hair which erupts in tendrils around her oval face. She is tall, broad-shouldered and long-waisted; she has long, long legs but she is more comfortable in a tracksuit and sneakers than the tailored clothes that will one day transform her into a truly elegant woman.

Julia lives with her parents and two younger sisters in a low-slung, modern home on three acres of scrubby bushland. The house reflects the family who live there – wooden floors, clean lines, no frills. Julia's older brothers are away at university. They've been hard to live up to. but like them she is a prefect as well as sports captain at the state school she attends. Her mother runs an accountancy business from home. Her father has a desk job in town but his passion is their small farm. Julia adores her brothers and her father and gets on well with her mum most of the time, but her sisters drive her crazy.

She speaks slowly in a lazy, husky voice and now and then she reaches into the air and extends her long body into a luxurious and curvaceous stretch. She then opens her eyes very wide as if she has suddenly remembered that this is not a ladylike thing to do.

If you didn't know better, you'd say Julia was a very sexy girl.

She is seventeen.

'Because I'm tall and I love sport, and everyone around here knows my brothers, people assume that I've always been like them, in other words, a bit of a tomboy. In actual fact, when I was little, I was a really girlie little girl. I had all these ringlets, you know? Mum always had my hair tied up in these huge ribbons which dangled over my face – you can see them driving me mad in all the family photos because my face is always all screwed up. Anyway, I loved dolls. I had this huge family of dolls: the father doll, the mother doll, the children dolls. I looked after them day and night, fed them, dressed them, took them for walks, protected them from the dogs (my brothers always had dogs), played make-believe families with them. I really loved my dollies, yeah.

I wonder if there's a psychological reason for that? What do you think? It wasn't as if I was building a better family than the one I had, because my olds have always been a pretty good team. Maybe I was just lonely. My brothers, Dave and Steve, they were always off doing their own thing. My sisters are a lot younger than me. By the time they came along I was almost in double figures. Mum and Dad must have been on a break for quite a while. Actually I think Mum had some sort of breakdown or something.

When I was little we didn't have this nice house. We lived in this shack of a place that was on the property when Dad bought it. Dad is a frustrated farmer. There's nothing he would like better than to spend his life riding the range, chewing grass and slapping brands on cattle. Instead he goes off in a shirt and tie five days a week and works off his frustration here at the weekends.

Back then my brothers and I all slept in one room. When the boys started growing up a bit, my parents put up a curtain between my bed and the boys'. I don't know why they bothered. I could still see everything if I wanted to. Boys bits and pieces are no mystery to me. Actually, I used to ask them about their dangly parts and they would just laugh and tell me what was for what. Once I dressed up their willies in dolls' dresses – little frilly lime skirts. They made them dance. Then they – their willies, I mean – stood up and danced all by themselves. We all nearly laughed ourselves stupid. Once they got to puberty they weren't so open about it. I remember they started going to the bathroom to get dressed and stuff. There's only a year between them so it all started happening about the same time. Mum took me aside about then and told me the facts of life. She just told me the lot, in one big long talk one night in her room. It was a bit confusing. Sometimes I've asked her for some revision points and she's okay with that. She's very down to earth, my mother. But in the meantime we had sex education at school and with the pictures and notes they gave us, it all fell into place.

I'm glad I heard it first from Mum, as a lot of my friends have never talked about sex to their parents at all, and they are the ones who are so obsessed with it all. Them and the ones who don't have brothers. They worry about it so much. I don't. I try not to worry about anything unless I have to; Dad says worry is a waste of time. I think Mum worries a lot more than she lets on, but she is a very quiet woman. She only talks when she has something to say.

Not long after the boys hit puberty we must have built this house because we've had rooms of our own for a long time now.

I've had boyfriends as far back as I can remember. I think my first one was when I was three. I've got photographs of me being pushed in my stroller by a really spunky little boy. I had boyfriends all through school, starting with kindergarten when Darren Wheatley used to bring me chocolate biscuits. I never let them kiss me or anything, not even when I got to high school. In primary school I would let them put their fingers up into my ringlets. That's as far as it ever went.

The thing is, I always compared them with my brothers and, like, there was never any comparison. My brothers are great. They are funny and they care about me and they work hard and train hard – they are SO fit. Honestly, I work so hard at my fitness but I can never get as fit as them. All the boys I've ever had as boyfriends start off pretending to be interested in me but, really, it's only themselves they are really interested in. How they feel, how they look, what they want. Dave and Stevie don't worry about all that crap. If something has to be done, they just get in there and do it. If something has to be said, they say it.

Mind you, I don't mean my brothers are perfect. They are total slobs and their taste in music is pretty pathetic. But, you know, everything is relative and compared with other boys they come out looking pretty good.

So there's no use talking to me about my sex life because I don't have one. I'm just not interested. Most of my friends feel the same as me but a couple have changed. As for people outside my group, I've seen them get boyfriends, get confused, get obsessed – and then get screwed. After that some of them stay together and some don't. But there are always problems. Sex never seems to make them happy.

At the moment I'm going out with Brett. He is really good-looking, although he is a bit shorter than me and I have to be careful about what shoes I wear when we go out. Brett is totally into sport, like me. I watch him play footy and he comes to see me play netball. We both play volleyball and tennis, and I train regularly at the pool as well. We go out one night a week, either to a party or to a movie or if there's nothing on we just hang out at my place with our other friends. We have a good time but we're not, like, obsessed with each other or anything. We both have heaps of other friends and other things to do. And there's all the study we have to do this year too.

Brett and I don't hold hands or cuddle much. If we go out at night or we are alone at home together, there's a fair bit of kissing. Brett is quite a good kisser. But we know when to stop, if you know what I mean. I usually stop first.

I started letting boys kiss me when I was about fourteen. I felt I was missing out on something, even though it never looks all that pleasant on the television. All that spit – you wonder where it goes. Anyway, I don't mind admitting I was totally wrong. Like – totally. Nothing beats a really good kiss. Unfortunately, however, a lot of boys have no idea. I mean, they have no idea how to do it, they just jam their tongues into your mouth and they think that's sexy – and then they race off and tell their friends that they gave Julia a tonguie! But they also have no idea how important a good kiss is. If I ever met a really good kisser – I mean a *really* good kisser – I might be tempted to let him go a bit further. Not all the way, but a bit further, you know? Only, it would have to be *really* good, it would have to make me feel as if I was melting like hot chocolate.

I have only felt like that once in my life and that was with a really gorgeous boy called James, who I met on an inter-school visit last year, when I was sixteen. Our school took a whole bunch of sporting teams up to the north coast and we were billeted in students' homes. It was so lovely up there and we had the most fabulous time. The best part of it all was James. The funny thing is, after what I was saying about being fit and everything, James was different to most of the boyfriends I've had. He wasn't all over me like a rash. In fact he didn't like me at all at first. He was really tall and skinny and he had this long, silky black fringe and huge dark eyes with eyelashes you could have *brushed*, honestly, they were *so* long. But he didn't play sport or anything. He was in the debating team.

I met him when I came off during the volleyball and he made some insulting remark about the players' brains being kept in their muscles. So I asked him how many times he had represented his school and he said 'forty-five', quick as a flash. Only, of course, he was talking about debating. Anyway, he just kept turning up all day, in his blazer and long school trousers, thinking he looked so suave, while I was all hot and red in the face from playing. We kept arguing and sniping at each other. It was a bit like *Gone with the Wind*, have you seen it? It's a love story but there is plenty of action. The lovers fight all the time but there is this mysterious attraction all the same. Anyway, that night the host school had a disco in honour of our visit. And there he was, white shirt, black pants, sort of gliding towards me, not even smiling. And you know what? He didn't tell me I looked nice, he didn't even ask me to dance, he just started dancing in front of me. Well I couldn't help myself. I had to start dancing. He was just *so* good. He was the best dancer I've ever seen. He could really move. Actually, I think you have to be quite fit to be a genuinely good dancer.

We danced for hours. I ignored all the other boys that night. I only wanted to dance with James. And then we went outside and he reached out and cupped my face in his two hands and pulled me slowly towards him and then he kissed me. Honestly, it was just the most incredible kiss. Slow, gentle, teasing, then longer and longer. Melted chocolate all right. I felt as if something was just running right through me. I felt as if we were just...*blending*, you know? Our bodies just fitted exactly together. Luckily, after about half an hour out there with James, all the parents' cars started arriving to pick us up. All I can say is, it's lucky old James is 500 kilometres away.

I wish he would write to me. I sent him an e-mail but he didn't reply.

My brothers would hate him.

Brett and I have talked about sex and I told him I'm just not interested. He's cool with that. Anyway, it would interfere with his training. I hope it stays this way, but it probably won't. A lot of the girls around here are so eager to get a guy, especially a good-looking one. So Brett will probably go with one of them, sooner or later. It doesn't fuss me. Well, it does, but not heaps. Anyway, I'm getting used to it. The way I look at it is, if they only want you so they can have sex with you, they are not worth having.

Masturbation? No, I don't do that. I mean – what would be the point?

Mum has pointed out that I've been very lucky in my life. Nothing bad has happened to me, unless you count the arrival of Tammy and Meredith, who were put on earth for the sole reason to make my life difficult. Seriously, as Mum says, a lot of the girls who go with boys have a lot of problems – divorced parents, fathers on the dole, brothers and sometimes even parents who drink or smoke dope. Mum says I don't have any excuse to behave badly.

Mum and Dad had this huge row recently because Mum found all these condoms in Dave's drawer and Dave has a steady girlfriend at uni and Mum realised that Dave must be having sex with Sandra. She was absolutely furious. Then Dad got furious back at her and said it was perfectly natural for a 21-year-old male to be sowing his oats and at least he had the sense to protect himself and the girl. But Mum said it was wrong wrong wrong and even though she had always been honest with us all about sex, Dave had let her down, and what sort of example was it to Tam and Merry and did that mean Dad wouldn't mind if Julia (that's me) started sleeping around? And Dad said Dave was not sleeping with Sandra under our roof and never would, unless he married her, so Tam and Merry wouldn't know about it and as for Julia, well that was different. "Why?" yells Mum. "Because she's special!" yells Dad. "And because she's a girl!" Which you must admit is pretty unfair.

So in other words I don't even think that adults know what the right thing is when it comes to sex.

The interesting thing is, though, that Dave and Sandra broke up a few weeks after that and Dave told me he wished they hadn't slept together. "It was like we were building up to that but after it was done there was nothing much else to aim for," he said. "And it made breaking up so much harder, because we had been so intimate."

I was really surprised to hear Dave use a word like "intimate".

Even though I've had heaps of boyfriends I have a better time with my brothers and their mates when they come home from uni than I do with kids my age. The boys in this town seem so young. I can't wait until I am old enough to go and get a job in the city. I'm not brainy enough for uni but I'm a hard worker and I want to work in the hospitality industry because that could lead to travel.

I've never wanted to have sex with anyone (except maybe James, but I only knew him for forty-eight hours and I would have to know him a lot better before I considered it). Two of my close friends have had sex with their boyfriends and it hasn't done them much good. I mean, it hasn't made the boys any nicer to them or anything. It hasn't given them security – quite the opposite in fact. Jan broke up with hers soon afterwards and Katie and Drew are still going out but they fight a lot because he is now very jealous.

The way I see it, your sex is all you've got. It's totally yours, it's unique, it's special. Once you've given it away, you never get it back. That's part of you gone forever.

The person you eventually share your sexuality with would have to be very very special and someone you were planning to share everything else with as well. I mean, I know I sound very old fashioned, but I really like the idea of making love to someone because you've decided to spend your whole life together – so that the first time is the beginning of everything.'

STDs: DISEASES YOU CAN
GET BY HAVING SEX

Masturbation is not the only subject young people don't wish to discuss, either with each other or with anyone else. The other unmentionable is the reality of becoming infected with a sexually transmissible disease, or STD, which happens to many sexually active girls and boys during adolescence. At least two of the young people who have told their stories in this book are being treated for STDs. Like most girls and boys, they didn't believe it could happen to them, they didn't want to talk about it, and for a long time they ignored the symptoms.

The least pleasant aspect of sexuality, apart from being caught with your pants down around your ankles, is catching an STD. Although most young people think that this could never happen to them, the only girls and boys who are totally safe from STDs are those who never do anything sexual with another person.

Research by the Centre for the Study of Sexually Transmissible Diseases at La Trobe University indicates that sexually active young people in Australia in the thirteen to nineteen age group are at high risk for STDs. In 1996, 20% of gonorrhoea cases were in that age group, as were 15% of acute hepatitis B infections, 14% of syphilis cases and 23% of chlamydia infections. A lot of adolescents get genital warts, genital herpes and non-specific urethritis.

Some kids say STDs are not as bad as you think. That depends on how you define bad. STDs are painful, messy, smelly, itchy and embarrassing and they can make people very ill as well as doing long-term damage to their reproductive systems.

The best way to avoid STDs once you become sexually active is to use a condom correctly every time you have vaginal, oral or anal sex.

Sticking to one sexual partner helps, but even then a boy or girl is still at risk if the other person has had other partners in the past

The contraceptive pill, taken correctly, will prevent girls from becoming pregnant but will not protect them from STDs.

Never EVER be embarrassed about insisting on protecting yourself from STDs. Everyone has the right to make sure that nothing itchy, painful, yucky, smelly and, in some cases, horribly dangerous and life threatening gets into their body.

Never share a needle or syringe – not even once. Putting a needle in your veins that has been in someone else's bloodstream means you expose yourself to a variety of diseases – including the HIV virus and hepatitis.

WHAT IS AN STD?

An STD is a disease that is passed from one person to another by sexual contact. Sexual contact can involve vaginal, anal or oral sex.

STDs range from a mild genital irritation to diseases that can cause infertility (the inability to make a baby) and serious illness. The best known STD is AIDS which is caused by a virus called HIV (human immunodeficiency virus). Like other STDs, HIV is contagious. AIDS itself is not contagious; it is a syndrome that can (but does not always) develop if a person has been exposed to the HIV virus. While there is no cure, it is no longer always fatal. There are positive management systems for people who are HIV-positive and those who have AIDS-related illnesses.

A big problem with STDs is that it's not always obvious when somebody has one. A lot of people look and feel healthy, even though they are carrying an STD infection or virus in their bodies. Young people who suspect they've been in contact with an infected person, or who have decided to have sex with a new partner, are advised to visit a doctor or health care worker (at medical centres or clinics like those run by Family Planning Australia) and ask for a checkup. This is not being dramatic. It's just being responsible about keeping in good health.

If they discover they have an STD, as embarrassing as it is, they are obliged to tell anyone with whom they've had sex, even if it was months ago. Otherwise they are putting the health of many others at risk.

COMMON STDs

NON-GONOCOCCAL URETHRITIS

Also called NGU or NSU, this is one of the most common STDs suffered by males. Symptoms include a slight white or cloudy discharge (not semen) from the penis and/or irritation or stinging when urinating (weeing). Infection usually appears two to four weeks after intercourse with an infected person. Sometimes there are no symptoms at all.

Without treatment, complications can cause chronic or permanent discomfort or pain in the penis and testicles.

Treatment: Antibiotics. No sex or alcohol for two weeks.

CHLAMYDIA

Women can have this infection for months and not know about it until a partner develops NGU as a result of her passing on the germ. Chlamydia has been called the 'silent epidemic'. If symptoms do appear they include a change in vaginal secretions, lower abdominal pains or abnormal vaginal bleeding. Chlamydia can cause PID – an inflammation in the Fallopian tubes which makes women infertile and/or causes pelvic pain.

Treatment: Antibiotics. Absolutely no sex or alcohol for two weeks.

GONORRHOEA (THE JACK, THE DRIP OR THE CLAP)

In women this may not cause any obvious symptoms, although there may be extra vaginal discharge or irritation when urinating. Men will notice a heavier, pus-like white or yellow discharge from the penis and/or a burning sensation when weeing. Infection in the rectum, caused by anal sex, may not cause noticeable symptoms. Infection through oral sex may cause a sore throat or no symptoms.

Gonorrhoea can cause infertility in women and pain and possible infertility in men.

Treatment: Antibiotics. No sex until follow-up tests prove that the disease is cured.

PELVIC INFLAMMATORY DISEASE (PID)

PID causes lower abdominal pain and tenderness, deep pain during intercourse, heavier, more painful periods and fever. The symptoms may not appear for weeks or months after infection. PID can damage the Fallopian tubes causing infertility and/or ectopic pregnancy, which occurs when a fertilised egg develops in the tubes, causing severe pain and internal bleeding and requiring urgent surgery.

Treatment: At least fourteen days of antibiotics plus follow-up checks. Hospital treatment may be necessary in serious cases. Recurrence is very serious.

GENITAL WARTS

Genital warts are tiny swellings on the genitals, sometimes developing into lumps like little cauliflowers; others are flatter. Some grow inside the vagina or on the cervix so that women are unaware of them. In men the warts generally grow on the penis. Warts can also appear around the anus. Usually painless, the warts sometimes go away but can also multiply.

Treatment: Women should have a pap smear. Genital warts can be removed by a doctor using freezing, burning or laser treatment but this won't get rid of the virus that causes them and they often come back. If untreated they can cause pre-cancerous changes in a woman's cervix. Tracing sexual contacts can be complicated because the warts take a long time before appearing.

GENITAL HERPES

Painful, tingling or itchy blisters or ulcers on the genitals or around the mouth (when they are called cold sores) can be accompanied by flu-like symptoms. Sometimes they are just red patches. They can appear within a few days or longer after getting the infection. The sores usually heal themselves but the virus stays in the system and they can recur even when there is no further contact with an infected partner.

Pregnant women should tell their doctor or midwife if they have had genital herpes so that precautions can be taken to prevent the disease from being given to the baby during childbirth.

Treatment: Tablets taken continuously reduce the number of outbreaks and heal early outbursts more quickly. No permanent cure.

TRICHOMONIASIS (TRIKE)

This is caused by a parasite which can be found in the female genital tract. Most men and women have few symptoms, although there may be a frothy, yellowish vaginal discharge. Trike is transmitted to women having unprotected vaginal sex with infected men. It can also be passed from woman to woman if there is vaginal discharge on the hands or on sex toys.

Treatment: A single dose of antibiotics is usually sufficient, with no alcohol for twenty-four hours after treatment. Pregnant women should tell their doctor.

SYPHILIS

A painless sore appears in the area of sexual contact in the early stages, ten to ninety days after infection, and usually clears up after two to six weeks, but the bacteria still remain. This may go unnoticed, especially by women, whose sores may occur on the walls of the vagina. In the second stage, seven to ten weeks after infection, there may be a rash on the palms of the hands or soles of the feet or other parts of the body.

Syphilis can affect any organ of the body. It used to be deadly but is now easily cured, although it is still highly contagious. If syphilis is left untreated it can progress to a third stage which results in insanity. Syphilis in pregnancy also has a devastating effect on the unborn child.

Treatment: Blood tests indicate whether the infection has been present for weeks, months or years. Antibiotic injections or tablets, ranging from ten to thirty days are usually effective.

PUBIC LICE (CRABS)

Tiny lice in the pubic hair cause itching. Anyone who has close body contact with the infected person can be affected.

Treatment: Head lice lotion from the chemist has to be applied from head to toes, left overnight and then washed off. This must be repeated in seven days. Clothing and bed linen must be washed in hot water to destroy lice and eggs. If itching persists, see a doctor.

SCABIES

Passed on through skin contact, scabies are tiny mites, smaller than crabs, which burrow under the skin to lay eggs, leaving fine red marks on the skin. They prefer warm areas, like the groin and armpits. The itching is unbearable and begins about four weeks after infection. Sexual partners and family members are at risk.

Treatment: Special lotions from the chemist must be applied from the neck down and the treatment should be repeated a week later. Clothes, bed linen and towels have to be washed in hot water.

MOLLOSCUM CONTAGIOSUM

These are little pimples which are firm, painless and waxy in appearance, caused by a virus transferred by skin contact. They appear in the genital area and other parts of the body two to seven weeks after contact has occurred.

Treatment: The pimples must be scraped to remove the core and painted with a special chemical. They may clear up by themselves but they may also spread.

HEPATITIS A

This virus affects the liver and is passed on in saliva and faeces (poo, shit). Symptoms include jaundice (yellow skin), dark urine, fever, stomach pain and fatigue.

Treatment: Bed rest for three weeks or more usually guarantees complete recovery.

HEPATITIS B AND HEPATITIS C

These viruses also affect the liver and can be passed on in body fluids such as semen, vaginal secretions, saliva and especially blood, which is why drug users who share equipment are particularly at risk.

Hep B and hep C can vary from a mild infection to a serious illness causing jaundice, fever, loss of appetite, lethargy and joint pains. Damage to the liver can lead to cirrhosis and liver cancer and may be fatal. Symptoms occur within three months of infection. The big problem with hep B and hep C is that people often don't realise what is wrong, assuming they are suffering from a bad bout of influenza. Even after recovery, the virus often remains in the system, damaging the liver and infecting others when sexually transmitted.

Treatment: Bed rest. Recovery is slow and, as sufferers can be carriers, follow-up blood tests are important. Hep B is the only STD for which there is a preventive vaccine, and doctors strongly recommend that all young adolescents are immunised. (This involves a course of three injections.)

A new drug has been discovered which may help in some cases. Specialist treatment is essential.

HIV AND AIDS

HIV is a virus that causes a lifelong infection which usually damages the body's immune system. AIDS occurs as a result of complications from the HIV infection. AIDS conditions include serious infections or cancers resulting from a damaged immune system which usually occur about ten years after the person has been infected with HIV. However, the time can vary from one to more than twenty years.

HIV is commonly transmitted by sharing needles or other drug-using equipment. It can also be spread by unprotected anal or vaginal intercourse. HIV can be passed by an infected mother to her baby during pregnancy, birth or breast feeding.

When a condom is properly used, HIV is rarely transmitted by vaginal or anal sex. It is not usually transmitted through oral sex (although ejaculation increases the risk), but the danger of infection increases if contaminated blood comes into contact with cuts and abrasions, or gets into the eyes.

HIV has never been reported as being transmitted by kissing, cuddling, or shaking hands, or by communal use of cutlery, crockery or toilets seats.

AFTERWARDS

It's normal to be pretty low if you've had an STD, even a mild one. The best thing a young person can do is to talk to someone about how they feel – their mum or dad, their doctor or perhaps a good friend or a youth counsellor.

Eating lots of fruit and vegies is a good idea, as is getting plenty of regular sleep and forgiving themselves – everyone is entitled to make a mistake from time to time.

NOT STDs, BUT NOT NICE

In girls and women, a healthy discharge from the vagina is quite normal. This is usually whitish in colour and dries into a yellowish stain on the pants. The discharge keeps the vagina healthy. Sometimes it is heavier than others. It has a particular smell which is not noticeable as long as people wash regularly.

Occasionally the vaginal discharge changes in a way that causes itching, soreness, or an unpleasant smell. It can also cause painful intercourse. If this happens, a visit to a doctor or health centre is recommended.

Some diseases are not sexually transmitted but still affect the genital area and should be treated.

THRUSH (CANDIDA)

This disease is not usually sexually transmitted so partners don't require treatment, although sex while affected is not a good idea. In women, an abnormal white or creamy yellow vaginal discharge with a yeasty odour is accompanied by inflammation of the skin around the vagina and intense itching. In men, thrush can develop on the foreskin and head of the penis as an itchy rash called 'balanitis'.

Thrush can be caused by using antibiotics, by diabetes, pregnancy, viral infections and excessive sweating; it is often caused by wearing tight nylon panties.

Treatment: Antifungal creams, pessaries (tablets which are inserted into the vagina) or oral tablets.

BACTERIAL VAGINOSIS (GARDNERELLA)

Not a sexually transmissible disease, this consists mainly of an unpleasant odour which may accompany a vaginal discharge. Symptoms can be more obvious after sex or during periods.

Treatment: Antibiotics.

That Saturday changed everything. Ben and Lucy saw less of each other at school – he hung out more with his mates and she started chatting about clothes and TV shows to Rebecca again. She decided that Ben was really very nice and no more inclined to bitchiness than she was herself.

They saw each other at weekends, but they went back to walking – not along the beach, just around the local parks and reserves. Kissing and cuddling had become too complicated and it was easier to just walk along, and hold hands, and talk. It was incredible how much they could always find to talk about. Ben loved to hear her laugh – that quaint, husky chuckle. She loved it when he smiled. He was so serious, most of the time.

They stopped fighting altogether.

At night he lay in bed and tried to think about her laugh, instead of remembering how it had felt to cup her soft little breast in his big hand. Magic. Unbelievable. Soft. Soft. Soft. He started changing his own bed sheets. Di didn't ask why.

They went to the movies. They went to a few parties and danced close. They sat in other people's rumpus rooms and talked about music and held hands. When other couples around them writhed and wrestled, they sat with their arms around each other and remained demure. They'd been there and done that. One night, at a party someone was giving because their parents were away, Ben drank too much and started climbing all over Lucy, kissing and pleading. She laughed at him and kissed him back and took him home to his mother who winked at her and said Ben didn't deserve her at all. Lucy felt much better about everything after that.

Ben didn't feel a lot better. He wondered how much it mattered, this sex business. Sometimes he thought he must be the only guy in his grade who hadn't done it. Other times he listened to what his mates were saying and felt fairly convinced that they were all in the same boat. Then he would look at Lucy and know in his heart that he would rather be with her than anyone else, with or without the sex. How weird.

The prunus trees lining Lucy's street turned pink with blossoms and the cricket season began. Ben's weekends were spent mainly at the pitch. Lucy told her father she wanted to go back to swimming training. She was a beautiful swimmer. She wanted to be good at something Ben would admire.

They made a special time each night to phone each other. They did their homework first, so Ben's parents couldn't complain. Lucy's father never complained about anything. But he had started making sure he was home to have dinner with her and Gregory every night. He told her quite often how lucky he was to have such a gorgeous daughter who not only had brains but could cook the best chilli meatballs in the southern hemisphere.

ONCE UPON A TIME: EVERYTHING CHANGED

(A CHAPTER MAINLY FOR PARENTS)

Look at us! We all wear jeans and sneakers. Half of us pierce our ears. We all have bad hair days. We all worry about our friends and traffic and the environment and not having enough money and getting fat! Are we really all that different to our kids?

It's commonly believed that when it comes to young people's relationships, parents and their adolescent children have totally different ideas. This myth is attributed to the seriously over-exposed 'generation gap'.

And yet, possibly without realising it, both generations are actually hoping for the same thing.

Parents want their children to be safe. Parents want their children to be happy. Parents want their children to have good and long-lasting relationships.

Young people want to be safe from unwanted pregnancy and sexually transmitted disease. Young people want to be happy. Young people want to have good and long-lasting relationships.

The differences lie in each generation's attitude to sexual relationships, which have altered quite dramatically over the last twenty years. But while the ground rules for sex have changed, the rules for love haven't changed at all and never will.

It is now acceptable to have casual sexual relationships, where previously this was frowned upon, even by adolescents themselves. Because of this sexual freedom, the health risks associated with sexual activity are greater than they have ever been.

The prospects for young men in society have changed. Becoming an adult man used to involve leaving school, getting a job, earning a good wage and, with that, preparing for a new range of responsibilities and achievable expectations, including long-term employment, marriage and children. Many young men no longer have these expectations; job security, a lasting marriage and a family of their own are no longer among life's certainties.

Young women's prospects have similarly altered, although most of them still count on having children at some stage. The position of women in society has changed dramatically but not completely; young women are now receiving some confusing and contradictory messages about how they should lead their lives.

Marriage used to be a rite of passage for young men and women. Then the sexual revolution rolled around and for many people the deeply meaningful nature of marriage slowly slipped away. It is now acceptable not to get married at all. Thousands of couples from every spectrum of society live in de facto relationships and have children.

Many of the rites and customs associated with marriage were crushed under the wheels of the revolution. Before the wedding, mothers were aware (albeit unwillingly) that if it hadn't already happened, one of those awkward, fluttery little talks about sexuality – or at least about contraception – was due. In our sexually permissive society, this no longer happens. How could it? Some daughters have been on the pill since starting high school. Some have been sharing their bed with their boyfriends since the age of fifteen. ('Well, it was obvious they were going to have sex anyway, so...' So what? So parents should supply clean sheets and home comforts and look the other way while their children put their physical and emotional development at risk?) Numerous couples marry after living together for years (and then, astonishingly, many of them divorce).

Confusion has occurred because, as is often the case with revolutions, no new rites of passage have been created to take the place of those once associated only with marriage.

Sexuality has been liberalised but there has been little education to go with it. Nobody knows what the rules are any more. And there must be rules, particularly in the rebellious phase of adolescence. *Without rules, the kids have nothing to rebel against – nor do they have anything to lean on or to protect them when they need time out.*

It's important to put these changes into context and to give young people the chance to think about the consequences. The best people to introduce these issues for discussion and consideration are parents.

SEX EDUCATION STARTS AT HOME

For many parents, sex education is just too hard. Some never attempt it at all. Others dutifully buy *Where Did I Come From?* and give it to their children to read. Many parents march their nine year olds off to sex education lectures organised through the school and come home with a feeling of relief that it's over and the job is done. They can cross it off, along with toilet training and immunisation shots. Mums and dads who sit down with their children and discuss sex and sexuality at regular intervals are very much in the minority.

Who can blame them? Even in our sexually liberated society, with people arching and thrusting on television screens in our lounge rooms every night of the week, with sex being used to sell everything from running shoes and jeans to cars and chocolate bars, talking about sex in a personal way is still a very difficult thing to do.

Today's parents are the first generation to supposedly benefit from the sexual revolution which rocked and rolled society during the sixties and seventies. Despite this, for many of them, the reality of their own adolescents' emerging sexuality is too much. It's too difficult, too embarrassing, too damn *soon*.

As their children grow up into sexual beings, many parents prefer to avert their flushed gaze and look at something else. As in our faces as sex has become, in many households there may be less talk about it now than there has ever been. The parents presume the kids know it all. The kids presume their parents know nothing. So it's never mentioned.

The truth, according to the people who work with them, is that kids are not as well informed about sex and sexuality as their parents believe. Sex education is now part of the personal development and health curriculum at most high schools, but anecdotal evidence suggests that students don't take a lot of notice of what they are taught in health class; those who are taking science might absorb a few more facts when they study reproduction.

Most teenagers get the information from their friends – but from where are their friends getting it? Some say they see it on television, but what they learn from the box is not likely to do them much good. They come away with the assumed knowledge that even a first kiss is not a kiss unless they are wagging their tongues around in someone's mouth and that this will quickly be followed by sexual intercourse during which all that is required for mad, passionate love is a comfortable bed and a condom.

TALKING TO KIDS ABOUT SEX AND STUFF

Talking about sex is embarrassing. For all age groups. Always has been. It's quite normal to feel awkward, but don't let that put you off. Grit your teeth, grin and bear it. Say the words. Ask the questions. Remember how you used to get up in the dead cold of night when they cried? Remember wearily changing the bed sheets at 3 am when they'd already thrown up twice and missed the sick bowl both times? Remember how you blamed yourself when they were injured, how toilet training drained your patience, how emotionally distraught you were when their friends rejected them? What's a little embarrassment compared to that? Think of sex talk as just another stage in the parenting adventure.

It's important to keep in mind some vital facts.

- Young people who talk with their families about sexuality and relationships are less likely to practise sex in unsafe, unwise or destructive ways.
- There are no wrong questions. (Although sometimes, because they are young, there is wrong timing.)
- If the kids are *not* asking questions, if none of them are talking about sex, it doesn't mean you are in the clear. It means it's up to you to initiate the discussion.
- If you are not willing to answer their questions about sex honestly, they won't ask you questions about drugs and other temptations.

- Just as kids who are well informed about drug and alcohol abuse are less likely to abuse these drugs, girls and boys who are well informed about sexuality are going to be safer in the choices they make.
- It's a myth that having the information will make them rush out and try it!

Sex has always fascinated people – why shouldn't it be discussed, in a general way, at the family dinner table or during a dreary trip in the car? Asking young people about what they believe is right and what is wrong with the way sexuality is practised in our society – or among their circle of friends – will open the doors to more complex discussion. Their opinions may even give you a pleasant surprise.

Sex in itself offers countless areas for discussion – from censorship to homophobia, from de facto marriage to nuptial mass, from prostitution to penis envy.

Some good general questions to ask include:

- How do you think life would change if you were involved in a sexual relationship?
- In a practical way, what does commitment involve?
- Why has the institution of marriage lasted so long?
- Why are de facto relationships so popular today?
- What is the best way to make up after a fight?

Parents should ask questions. They should also be prepared to answer their kids' questions. If they don't know some of the answers, they should say so. There's always the library or the internet.

It is much harder bringing up children in an era when people's interpretation of values is so much more fluid than it was in the more rigid past. It was simpler for parents when everyone in their community agreed that sex before marriage was just plain wrong. On the other hand, those 'good old days' were responsible for the misery of shotgun weddings, butchered abortions and terrible shame and heartbreak too. It is also an inescapable fact that through the ages, many young people, regardless of public and/or religious opinion, have always regarded the rules against having sex as being there to be broken.

Nevertheless, every parent has the right to ask their children to respect the family's moral standards. Many religions and cultures hold the view that sex and procreation are permissible only within the sanctity of marriage. If that is your belief, your children will obviously be aware of this from an early age. In families where there are no strict guidelines on morality issues, the question of sex is less straightforward. For many people, the issue of right and wrong is a very personal one.

Talking about sex with adolescents doesn't mean insisting that they agree with you. Whatever they say won't make much difference anyway once they fall in love with some gorgeous young thing. (The parents may not think the young thing is gorgeous, but that's just the point.) But adults are not required to change their minds either. And the kids don't want them to, not really. It's more important that their parents are not hypocritical in their opinions and that they practise what they preach.

BUILDING BOUNDARIES

More important than anything is the need for parents to set boundaries for their children and to be around to ensure those boundaries are doing the job.

As children grow into adolescence, the boundaries need to be redefined. But they should still be there and parents need to ensure that these lines are recognised and respected. No matter how much the kids whinge and whine about everybody else's parents being much more broadminded than theirs; and no matter how loudly they moan or how silently they sulk or how irritatingly they shout and shake their razored number ones or their tousled mops, they want those limits. They need them.

With boundaries in place – or you can call them rules, or limits, or standards, or values, whatever you like – kids have an established line against which they can rebel. It's a line that enables them to make decisions about their lives. They can take risks that will shock their parents. They can go very close to the edge without falling over.

Without boundaries the risks become more dangerous. If their parents are neither interested nor involved, or if they are interested but too distracted, busy or easy-going, kids are much more likely to try to impress their friends rather than their families. It takes a lot more to shock a kid than a parent. Dangerous risks can involve drink and drug abuse, which turns peer pressure into a life-threatening game, or casual sex. Having indiscriminate sex doesn't only risk illness and pregnancy; it may also cause pain, confusion, rejection, disappointment and hurt, which can and often does last a lifetime.

Peer pressure is the biggest problem when it comes to setting boundaries – not only theirs, but yours. The spectre of Everybody Else's Parents haunts most households and undermines many parents' confidence in their own judgment. Be reassured. Everybody Else's

Parents, those broadminded, generous creatures who scorn curfews, hand out unlimited allowances, ignore MA ratings on videos, go away almost every weekend and install phone lines and television sets exclusively for their teenagers' use, are actually a very rare breed. They do exist but only in isolated pockets, and they rarely come out in the daylight. The best possible way to fight the spectre is not with a cross or a stake but with a phone call. Getting to know the parents of your kids' friends, and discovering that they set boundaries too, is an effective and reassuring way of keeping in touch with what is going on in the lives of your adolescent children.

If for no other reason, boys and girls need boundaries so they can break them down when the time comes for them to grow up and go. Which they will, all too soon.

WHY SEX ISN'T GOOD FOR KIDS (SORRY KIDS)

A lot of young people are very anxious about getting a boyfriend or a girlfriend. But those who enter into a sexual relationship often become even more worried. Most of them don't enjoy the sex anywhere near as much as they thought they would. Apart from that, they become discontented fairly easily. They get very upset when things don't seem to be working out. They become depressed. When their relationships fail, some even attempt or commit suicide.

Many teenagers are not handling their relationships well. They don't know how. They are not mature enough to handle the negotiation and communication that is involved in a sexual commitment. In adolescence, young people are the victims of their own hormones and their moods swing to extremes; they are not always prepared for discussion and compromise, either with their parents or their lovers, and whether young couples stay together can be decided on a whim or impulse which may be deeply regretted.

Parents can and do warn teenagers of the risk of disease and unwanted pregnancy. If their young people have been properly educated, they will claim that safe sex practice prevents both. But there is another, less visible reason why sexual relationships are not advisable for adolescents. Sex adds layers and layers of complications to a relationship. The risks of heartbreak and tragedy are increased. Because they are young and inexperienced, teenagers don't understand the emotional damage that sex can do. This doesn't just apply to girls. When a sexual relationship breaks down, boys fall very hard too. The difference is that they don't talk about it They take refuge in anger and vulgarity or deep, hostile silence, and their depression is easily misunderstood even by those who love them best.

Short-term sexual affairs may sentence young people to a lifetime of similar relationships, in which they equate love only with physical sexual acts, robbing themselves of the security and affection that come with companionship and commitment.

TROUBLED YOUNG PEOPLE

Marginalised and troubled young people are even less likely to be able to handle the issue of sexuality. These are the boys and girls who have been sexually or physically abused, who have come from broken and battling homes, or who are homeless and living on the streets. They include young people who have behavioural problems, mental health problems and drug addiction; they are kids who have experienced trauma, distress and intense grief during their childhood and adolescence.

Young people with no framework to guide them are incredibly disadvantaged. They over-indulge themselves with sex, drugs and alcohol, and as a result they stagger from one stupid and harmful risk to another, often taking others with them in their journey to self-destruction. They elicit little pity from the community and yet they deserve sympathy rather than blame. They've never been taught. Nobody has cared enough about them to demonstrate the right way to behave in society, to bring them back from the edge on which they have balanced precariously for as long as they can remember.

With support, with good counselling and practical help, many of these young people have proved that they can overcome their problems. Research has shown that if troubled young people believe that just one adult in their lives really cares about them, their self-esteem, confidence and energy is likely to increase.

Mental health counsellors, community health and youth workers, priests and ministers of religion and some school teachers are working with disadvantaged boys and girls in ways that can quite quickly turn their lives in a more positive direction. There are not enough of these people and it's not surprising. Their salaries are not handsome, their safety is often threatened and most of them look worn-out. It's a tough job but perhaps more people would do it if their efforts were recognised, respected and more appropriately rewarded. Their work is appreciated by many of their clients but they can't pay their bills with gratitude.

THE BOREDOM FACTOR

It might sound trite, hackneyed and predictable, but there's no doubt that boredom can lead to early sexual activity. Even for young people, sex takes up a lot of time. Girls and boys who lead busy, interesting lives are far less likely to be tempted into mucking around with sexual experimentation (or, for that matter, drugs).

We live in an age of extra-curricular activities, when three year olds are carted off to ballet class as soon as they can stumble around on their porky little pointers, and parents take on second jobs to pay for the music lessons, the sporting fees, the academic coaches and a whole host of other excursions and carefully devised learning experiences. A lot of children barely have time to play any more and day-dreaming has to be scheduled between language classes and soccer practice.

And yet the minute puberty gets under way, just when young people could do with some activities to distract them from their new obsession with themselves and the opposite sex, enthusiasm wanes. Girls lose interest in sport, boys lose interest in scouts and soccer and parents lose interest in providing a taxi service for this suddenly large, loud and ungrateful mass of heaving young hormones. Without the continued interest and encouragement of parents, young people are much more likely to turn to their friends for attention.

In the words of former Crowded House singer Neil Finn, talking to *Good Weekend* magazine about kids in New Zealand: 'It's a wasteland out there for young people. Apart from the ones who have very interested parents who keep their kids involved in good things, there's a lot of kids wandering around with nowhere to go and no-one giving them opportunities to be expressive or creative.'

It's not much different in the suburbs and towns of Australia.

A lot of teenagers get casual jobs. Having been brought up in families where material acquisitions have become the highest priority, the pursuit of money of their own becomes more important to young people than sport or even having fun. When it comes to sport, hobbies and culture, we are starting – and consequently finishing – far too early. This is unfortunate, because it is during adolescence that kids can *really* benefit from being busy.

WHERE TO GO, WHAT TO DO?

From the age of around thirteen, when they are finally old enough to go out alone with their friends, right through until young people can legally get into pubs and clubs at eighteen, there is very little youth-oriented entertainment available, apart from movie cinemas. Depending on who holds them, dance parties and teenage discos tend to be associated with either religious organisations or, at the other end of the social scale, drug trafficking. If boys want to meet girls, where do they go? If a boy and girl want to spend time together, where do they go, what do they do?

They mainly go to the shopping centres, those gleaming new village greens of community life, where consumers are always welcome but kids without dollars are not. Not that this keeps them away.

'In my day...' say the parents, 'we were never bored.' In their day what did they do? They went dancing. They went on picnics. They went to the beach. They went to the movies. They played sport. So do kids today, when they can find a dance they're allowed into, when they can talk their parents into letting them catch the bus and the train all the way to a beach, when they can find enough parents willing to take time out from their own frantic job-driven lives to drive them to a picnic place. Some play music. Some play sport. These provide great ways to meet other boys or girls – but then what? What do they do? Where do they go?

Is it any wonder that suburban teenagers' parties are inundated with numbers far beyond their expectations? It's reputed that the kids just get together to get drunk, but at most of these gatherings the numbers who binge are much lower than those who are there simply because it's somewhere to be with their friends on a Saturday night.

A hugely successful Anglican youth group which operated for years in Sydney's west, attracting between 200 and 300 twelve to eighteen year olds every week, was forced to temporarily close its doors when the premises it rented for next to nothing were torn down to make way for 'Australia's biggest cinema complex'. The boys played pool and basketball there, the girls used to play games and chat and as they all grew older and became interested in the opposite sex, they had a place where they could get to know each other. Highlights of the annual program included camping trips and beach parties. Regardless of their religious affiliations, if any, everyone was welcome. Everyone went.

'They wouldn't go,' is a cop out. Of course the kids would go. As long as their friends are there, any place but school is a cool place to be.

Governments would save millions of dollars of rescuing money (currently going out on health, pensions, legal aid and juvenile crime) if some preventive measures, in the form of youth centres, were an integral part of our community. Well designed, staffed by energetic young and young-at-heart people, offering a place to gather and an attractive program of events, such centres could also provide the essential information that young people need when it comes to sexual awareness, drug education and family problems.

Ideally, tucked away somewhere past the pool table or in the region of a steaming urn would be a room where a full-time resident counsellor could talk to troubled young people. In *Leaving Early*, a book about youth suicide in Australia, concerned teenagers suggested that a youth counselling service should exist in every suburb and every country town. What could be a better place for such a service than a place kids would call their own?

CONCLUSION: THE *BEST* THING

So who are the sluts and studs of the adolescent community? Where is the teenage boy, desperate to divest himself of his virginity, ready to root and run, eager to boast of his virility and swap seduction statistics with his mates? And where is his counterpart, the sloe-eyed seductress, tempting young men to stray into the moist warmth of her web, lying back and leading them to ruin, hoping for babies that will provide her with an escape from school and bless her with the riches of the supporting parents' pension?

Neither of them can be found within these pages.

Instead there are only boys and girls looking for love, hoping that somewhere out there, someone special is waiting for them.

The real challenge for most young people is finding someone who will be their best friend as well as their lover, a boy or girl who will provide strength when they need someone to lean on, who will care about them when they are in trouble and who will rejoice for them when they are happy.

In the meantime, in a world where everything seems to be changing, who can blame adolescents for grabbing at the first strands of sexual love they find and weaving themselves a synthetic blanket, wanting to believe it's genuine, hoping it will give them warmth and protection from the chilly winds of uncertainty, confusion and loneliness?

And when, eventually, they are forced to realise that the blanket isn't as warm and comforting as they had hoped, why should they be criticised for discarding it for another, and then another, as they keep on searching for something of better quality?

Isn't that what many adults have been doing for the past thirty years?

Good marriages and lasting relationships create a great deal of happiness. They are worth every minute of the patience, the pain, the heartache, the worry, the tolerance, the endurance, the laughter and the loving care we put into them. How much of that is what our sons and daughters are seeing today when they take a long look at their own families?

Most parents would prefer it if their children didn't have sex until they were grown up, married and paying off their own mortgages, or if that's too much to ask, at least off their P plates, managing their own Medicare cards and hand-washing their own brand-name clothes.

However, the number of young people who will follow their parents' wishes regarding their sex lives is probably roughly equal to the number of them who believe that Mum and Dad have had sex since their last child was conceived.

What the kids do absorb, whether they are aware of it or not, is the way they are loved and respected.

Before our children learn about sex and sexuality they need to learn about love. Growing up in a home where the adults love and respect each other, where every child knows with absolute certainty that he or she is loved and valued, where humour, even amid the most disastrous developments, is never too far away and where nobody – *NOBODY* – has the right to hurt another person – gives every young person a flying start in the sexual stakes.

This may be harder in some families than others. In single parent families, in blended and step families (particularly warring ones), two-way communication (talking *and* listening), open and honest discussion of problems and the setting of boundaries may be a lot more difficult. On the other hand, if these general principles are recognised, young people are more likely to enter relationships with the confidence and ability to make intelligent choices; they are less likely to be influenced by the complications that have dogged their parents.

In families where language barriers, cultural differences, unemployment, chronic illness, disability and poverty make life a battle for survival rather than a search for satisfaction, the challenge is greater, but still possible. Love costs nothing. Young people who are secure in the love and affection of their parents, or at least one of their parents, and even those who know they are loved and cared for by one caring, constant, reliable older person, are more likely to be selective and sensible about the way they manage their sex lives.

Every parent can try.

Every mother can tell her daughter she is special. She can tell her she has the right to control what happens to her body, that nobody has the right to force her to have sex, that her body is prone to pain but is capable of giving her infinite pleasure.

She can tell her son that he is special. She can tell him that strength of mind, and respect for himself and others will make him the best kind of stud – a boy who is selective and responsible about his sexuality and who cares about the young woman who might eventually become his lover and partner.

Every father can try. He can tell his daughter she is special. He can tell her she is lovely, that any boy on whom she bestows her favours is a lucky bloke and that she should take care to choose someone who is truly deserving of her unique and wonderful self.

He can tell his son that he is special. He can tell him that girls are unusual and unfathomable creatures who need a lot of care, respect and understanding because they think so differently to men. He can tell him not to rush into sexual encounters with girls just for the sake of proving his studliness – that he deserves the best and that the girls worth having are worth waiting for; that getting to know a girl can be an experience that is as rewarding as it is confusing – but well worth it in the end.

We can all try. We can all try just a little bit harder than we are doing now.

Adolescents as well as grown men and women have been fascinated by love and loving and sex and sexuality since the beginning of time. But if you are a young person on the brink of a sexual relationship, think carefully about how much your relationship with this boy or this girl means to you. Wonder how you are going to feel afterwards – not about the other person, but about yourself.

Think of your sexuality as a little bud inside your body. It has never seen the sunlight, but it's there, waiting for the right time, the right conditions, the right amount of loving care. One day one lover will find the bud and make it grow, and the petals of feeling will unfold and unfold in a way that will make you feel mysterious, marvellous, passionate, brilliant, warm and wonderful.

Love has often been likened to a rose. But when it happens to you, at a good time, in the best way, with the right person, it will be better and more beautiful than any flower you've ever seen.

Why would that be so wonderful? Because like just about everything that's good in life, sex is best when it's shared with someone you know well, someone you love and trust – and someone who trusts and loves you back.

Sex, when it happens in a loving, trusting, caring relationship, is the best and most beautiful act that a man and woman perform together.

But it's never simple.

The guys asked Ben how much progress he was making but he said he didn't want to talk about Lucy behind her back.

'Why?' asked Tom.

'Because she's my friend,' said Ben. Afterwards he thought about it. Lucy was his friend. She was the best friend he had ever had.

When school broke up for the spring holidays the sun dazzled itself into confusion and mistook the season for summer. Lucy and Ben caught the train to the beach, along with hundreds of others. They hit the waves running and laughing and the water snatched the breath from their lungs and laughed back at them. Ben plunged under wave after wave but every time he surfaced, Lucy was there beside him, water streaming from her hair. They swam out beyond the breakers, Ben ploughing through the waters like a big shaggy bear, Lucy stroking smoothly and strongly, her pale skin and no-colour hair gleaming.

'I love this,' she gasped. 'I love it so much.'

Ben was bursting with delight. Here was something really huge they had in common. The beach! Mum had always said he was born with salt water in his blood. And now here was Lucy, loving it too.

'I love you,' he yelled, but a massive wave crashed over them both, drowning out his words.

Afterwards they flung themselves down on their towels and let the first sunshine of summer dry them. They rested their faces on their warming arms and gazed sideways at each other, not touching, just looking. She had a lovely body, he thought. She was the perfect shape for a girl. It seemed such a long time since he'd first thought that. So much had happened.

'Lucy in the sky with diamonds,' he said. 'That's you. Diamonds in your eyes. Diamonds on your eyelashes.' He'd been practising saying it for a week. The diamonds in her eyes part, anyway. The diamonds on her lashes was a spark of brilliance, because that's what it looked like just then. Drops of water sparkling on her face.

'I'm so glad I met you,' said Lucy softly. She never needed to practise. She simply spoke the truth.

Ben smiled. He reached out and with one long finger, slowly traced the shape of a heart on her cheek. Lucy lay still.

'I want to make love to you,' said Ben. 'I dream about it all the time.'

Lucy put her hand over his finger and held it still against her cheek. She couldn't concentrate while it was moving. 'I know,' she murmured. 'It's going to be perfect. It's going to be like the best movies we've ever seen.'

'Oh no,' said Ben seriously. 'It's going to be much better. Movies don't last. Love does. See Lucy, I've been thinking a lot about this. It was getting too hard before and it was because all we were thinking about all the time was the sex. Now we're friends again. Best friends. And you know, like. . .it's better.'

Lucy gazed at him. 'I've never had a best friend,' she said softly.

'I've had heaps,' said Ben, 'but never one like you.'

Ben's index finger still lay against her cheek. She curled her own small fingers around it and slowly moved it to her lips. Ben put his face down into his arms and thanked God he was lying on his stomach.

'Lucy,' he mumbled. 'Have you any idea at all what that does to me?'

Lucy's sexy laugh teased at him. 'Yeah,' she said. 'I do.'

He kept his body very still, but he raised his face to turn towards her again. All his dreaminess had disappeared and he looked almost angry. 'Don't muck me about, Lucy,' he said. 'Before you seemed as keen as me. Keener, in fact. Now I don't know what is going to happen. I can't tell how you feel any more.'

She took his finger out of her mouth. 'I think that one day we will probably make love to each other,' she said slowly. 'It's just that I think we'll have to be older and smarter and a lot more independent than we are now. We don't want to hurt anyone. We don't want to let anybody down. Especially not each other.'

'I wouldn't want to hurt you, Lucy,' said Ben. 'But ...'

She smiled her wonderful smile and reached out to put a finger on his lips. 'But you know what, Ben? I honestly can't imagine feeling any happier with you than I'm feeling right now.'

'Well yeah, but I'm really looking forward to finding out,' he said, forcing a laugh, trying not to sound too desperate.

'I'm really looking forward to another swim.'

They jumped up quickly and raced into the sea together.

Lucy was thinking it would have been a perfect shot for the cameras, except that Ben was forced to run like an old man and because she was giggling at him, she cut her toe on a sharp shell. So this time they didn't hit the water running. They splattered in among the paddling children and the old ladies in bathing caps and they flopped about and laughed themselves silly.

Their long hot summer had barely begun.

|||| T H E   E N D ||||

THE NSW CENTRE FOR THE ADVANCEMENT OF ADOLESCENT HEALTH

The Department of Adolescent Medicine at the Royal Alexandra Hospital for Children has been at the forefront of developments in the field of adolescent health for the past two decades. As well as establishing a comprehensive, integrated and creative model of adolescent health care linking in-patient, outpatient and community services, the Department has undertaken focused research and provided undergraduate and postgraduate education and training at state, national and international levels.

Building upon this pioneering work, the NSW Centre for the Advancement of Adolescent Health at the New Children's Hospital seeks to improve the health and health care of young people and their families in New South Wales, Australia and beyond.

OBJECTIVES

- Develop guidelines for best practice in the delivery of health and medical care to young people and their families;
- Conduct and coordinate community development projects and applied research to advance the health and health care of young people and their families;

- Undertake interdisciplinary education and training for adolescent health workers and other professionals involved with the care and support of young people and their families;
- Facilitate local, national and international networks in support of adolescent health and health care;
- Contribute to the development, implementation and review of policies relevant to the health and health care of young people and their families.

A percentage of the royalties from the sale of this book will go towards the Centre to fund further research into adolescent health.

THE TOP TEN QUESTIONS ASKED ABOUT SEX

The following questions about sex and sexuality are among those most frequently asked by young people. Dr Melissa Kang, a specialist in adolescent health at the New Children's Hospital, Westmead, NSW, has provided the answers.

Q1: 'I've never had sex but sometimes I wake up at night feeling so horny it hurts. My vagina throbs. Is this normal?'

A: 'Absolutely. It's your reproductive system revving up its motor. But you don't have to go anywhere until you are ready.'

Q2: 'How can someone you're having sex with tell if you are a virgin?'

A: 'They can't.'

Q3: 'Can a penis be too small for having sex or too big to go into the vagina?'

A: 'Penis size makes no difference to sexual performance. No penis is bigger than a baby and a baby fits through a fully grown vagina so a penis cannot be too big. The vagina has elastic walls.'

Q4: 'Is it natural for women to have one breast bigger than the other?'

A: 'Yes. Our bodies are not symmetrical and no paired parts are identical in size.'

Q5: *'What is a wanker?'*

A: '"Wanker" is a derogatory term for someone who masturbates. Masturbation in private is a normal and healthy thing to do.'

Q6: *'Can you get an STD if you've only ever had sex with the one person?'*

A: 'Yes, but that person would have to be infected first for you to catch it.'

Q7: *'Can showering after unsafe sex stop you falling pregnant?*

A: 'No. Sperm are great swimmers and will swim strongly against gravity or rushing water to reach the female egg.'

Q8: *'Does having sex if you are more than seven months pregnant hurt the baby?'*

A: 'If the woman and her baby have been well throughout the pregnancy, having sex is quite safe. However, catching an STD in pregnancy can be harmful, so a condom should still be used, particularly if a new partner is involved.'

Q9: *'Can you get breast cancer and cervical cancer before you have sex?'*

A: 'Breast cancer, yes. Cervical cancer – probably not.'

Q10: *'Is it all right to have sex the first time you go out?'*
A: 'No.'

RESOURCES AND
RECOMMENDED READING

An excellent number of books and booklets on all aspects of sex education are available from Family Planning centres around Australia.

Family Planning Australia
9/114 Maitland Street
Hackett ACT 2602
Ph: *(02) 6230 5255*
Fax: *(02) 6230 5344*
Email   *fpa@actonline.com.au*

Family Planning ACT
Health Promotion Centre
Childers Street
(GPO 1317)
Canberra ACT 2601
Ph: *(02) 6247 3077 (clinic)*
          (02) 6247 3018 (education)
Fax: *(02) 6257 5710*
Email: *fpact@atrax.net.au*

Family Planning NT
Shop 11
Rapid Creek Shopping Centre
Trower Road
Rapid Creek NT 0810
Freecall™: 1800 193 121
Ph: *(08) 8948 0144*
Fax: *(08) 8948 0626*
Email: *fpnt@ozemail.com.au*

Family Planning Queensland
100 Alfred Street
Fortitude Valley QLD 4006
Ph: *(07) 3252 5151 (clinic)*
         (07) 3252 7922 (education)
Fax: *(07) 3854 1277*
Email: *fpq@powerup.com.au*

Family Planning TAS
2 Midwood Street
Newtown TAS 7002
(GPO Box 77 North Hobart TAS 7002)
Ph: *(03) 6228 5244 (clinic)*
Fax: *(03) 6228 1222*
Email: *Famplan.Hobt@tassie.net.au*

Family Planning NSW
328–336 Liverpool Road
Ashfield NSW 2131
Ph: (02) 9716 6099
Fax: (02) 9716 6164

Family Planning VIC
901 Whitehorse Road
(PO Box 1377)
Box Hill VIC 3128
Ph: (03) 9257 0100 (administration)
*   (03) 9257 0123 (clinic)*
Fax: (03) 9257 0112 (administration)
Email: fpv < fpv@smart.net.au >

Family Planning WA
70 Roe Street (PO Box 141)
Northbridge WA 6865
Ph: (08) 9227 6177
Fax: (08) 9227 6871
Email: sexhelp@fpwa-health.org.au

FURTHER READING

Secondary Students, HIV/AIDS and Sexual Health, 1997, by Jo Lindsay, Anthony Smith and Doreen Rosenthal, Monograph Series No 3, published by the Centre for the Study of Sexually Transmissible Diseases, Faculty of Health Sciences, La Trobe University, 1997.

Growing Pains: What To Do When Your Children Turn into Teenagers, by Dr David Bennett, Doubleday, Sydney, 1995.

Teenagers: A Guide to Understanding Them, by Terry Colling and Janet Vickers, Bantam Books, Sydney, 1988.

The Teenage Survival Book, by Sol Gordon, Times Books, USA, 1988.

Why Love is Not Enough, by Sol Gordon, Bob Adams Inc, USA, 1990.

When Living Hurts, by Sol Gordon, Dell Publishing, USA, 1988.

Anna's Story: Anna Wood – the Facts, the Fury, the Future, by Bronwyn Donaghy, Angus & Robertson, Sydney, 1996.

Leaving Early: Youth suicide – the Horror, the Heartbreak, the Hope, by Bronwyn Donaghy, HarperHealth, Sydney, 1997.

BOOKS ABOUT PREGNANCY AND BIRTH

Where Did I Come From? The Facts of Life Without any Nonsense and With Illustrations by Peter Mayle and Arthur Robins, Pan Macmillan, Sydney.

Having a Baby: The Essential Guide to Pregnancy and Birth, by Carol Fallows, Transworld, Sydney, 1997.

Baby Love, by Robin Barker, Pan Macmillan, Sydney, 1998.

Only the Beginning: Young Women's Stories about Pregnancy, Birth and Being a Mum, published by the Waterloo Girls Centre and South Sydney Youth Services, 1997.

Dear Nobody, a novel by Berlie Doherty, HarperCollins, Sydney, 1993.

BOOKS ABOUT HOMOSEXUALITY

Young, Gay and Proud, by Sasha Alyson, Alyson Publishing, Boston, 1985.

Am I Blue? Coming Out From the Silence, by Marion Dane Bavel, HarperCollinsPublishers, New York, 1994.

Now That You Know, by Betty Fairchild and Nancy Hayward, Harcourt Brace Jovanovich, New York, 1979.

Two Weeks With the Queen, a novel by Morris Gleitzman, Pan MacMillan, 1990.

Ready or Not? by Mark McLeod, Random House, Sydney, 1996.

My Child is Gay, by Bryce McDougall, Allen & Unwin, 1998.

INDEX